Sizzling MEXICAN RECIPES

Salsas & Snacks   2

Sassy Salads & Sides   24

Soups, Stews & Chilies   44

Tacos, Enchiladas & More   60

Mexican Main Dishes   90

Acknowledgments   121

Index   122

Salsas & Snacks

◆ 🌵 ◆

Mexican Chicken Skewers with Spicy Yogurt Sauce

1 package (1.25 ounces) taco seasoning mix, divided

6 boneless skinless chicken breast halves (about 1½ pounds), cut into 1-inch cubes

1 large clove garlic

¼ teaspoon salt

2 tablespoons olive oil

1 cup DANNON® Plain Nonfat or Lowfat Yogurt

1 red bell pepper, cut into chunks

1 green bell pepper, cut into chunks

1 yellow bell pepper, cut into chunks

In a large bowl combine 3 tablespoons seasoning mix and chicken; toss to coat well. Cover; chill 2 hours.

To make Spicy Yogurt Sauce, in a mortar and pestle or with a large knife, press garlic and salt together until a smooth paste forms. Place in a small bowl with olive oil; mix well. Stir in yogurt and remaining taco seasoning mix. Cover; chill 30 minutes before serving.

Thread chicken onto skewers alternately with peppers; grill over hot coals 10 to 12 minutes, turning occasionally. Serve with Spicy Yogurt Sauce. *Makes 12 servings*

NOTE: *If using wooden skewers, soak in water 30 minutes before serving. This will prevent skewers from charring and crumbling.*

Mexican Chicken Skewers with Spicy Yogurt Sauce

Fresh California Tomato-Pineapple Salsa

3 cups fresh California
    tomatoes, diced
1 cup fresh diced
    pineapple
⅔ cup sliced green onions
1 fresh jalapeño pepper,
    seeded and finely
    chopped

3 tablespoons chopped
    fresh cilantro
3 tablespoons fresh lemon
    juice
2 cloves garlic, finely
    chopped

Combine all ingredients in large bowl. Stir gently until evenly mixed. Serve salsa with grilled or broiled fish or chicken.

Makes 8 servings

Favorite recipe from **California Tomato Board**

Mexi Chex®

¼ cup margarine or butter
1 package (1.25 ounces)
    taco seasoning mix,
    divided
4½ cups Corn CHEX® brand
    cereal
1 pound ground beef
1 small head lettuce,
    shredded

2 medium tomatoes,
    chopped
1½ cups (6 ounces) shredded
    Cheddar cheese
Salsa
Sour cream

1. Melt margarine in microwave-safe bowl on HIGH 45 to 60 seconds. Stir in ½ package (2 tablespoons) seasoning mix. Add cereal, stirring until all pieces are evenly coated. Microwave on HIGH 2 minutes, stirring every minute.

2. Brown ground beef in large skillet over medium-high heat; drain. Stir in remaining ½ package seasoning mix and ¼ cup water. Simmer 5 minutes, stirring occasionally.

3. Layer 4 cups cereal, ground beef, lettuce, tomatoes and cheese in serving dish. Top with remaining ½ cup cereal. Serve with salsa and sour cream.

Makes 6 to 8 servings

Fresh California Tomato-Pineapple Salsa

Festive Chicken Dip

1½ pounds boneless skinless chicken breasts, finely chopped (about 3 cups)
¼ cup lime juice, divided
2 garlic cloves, minced
1 teaspoon salt
½ teaspoon ground black pepper
1 can (16 ounces) refried beans
1½ cups sour cream, divided
1 package (1¼ ounces) dry taco seasoning mix, divided
1 tablespoon picante sauce

1 avocado, chopped
1 tablespoon olive oil
1 cup (4 ounces) shredded sharp Cheddar cheese
1 small onion, finely chopped
2 tomatoes, finely chopped
1 can (2¼ ounces) sliced black olives, drained and chopped
1 bag (10 ounces) tortilla chips
Fresh cilantro for garnish

Place chicken in small bowl. Sprinkle with 3 tablespoons lime juice, garlic, salt and pepper; mix well. Set aside.

Combine beans, ½ cup sour cream, 2½ tablespoons taco seasoning and picante sauce in medium bowl. Spread bean mixture in bottom of shallow 2-quart casserole dish.

Combine avocado and remaining 1 tablespoon lime juice in small bowl; sprinkle over bean mixture. Combine remaining 1 cup sour cream and 2½ tablespoons taco seasoning in small bowl; set aside.

Heat oil in large skillet over high heat until hot; add chicken in single layer. Do not stir. Cook about 2 minutes or until chicken is brown on bottom. Turn chicken and cook until other side is brown and no liquid remains. Break chicken into separate pieces with fork. Layer chicken, sour cream mixture, cheese, onion and tomatoes over avocado mixture. Top with olives. Refrigerate until completely chilled. Serve with chips. Garnish with cilantro.

Makes 8 cups dip

Favorite recipe from **National Broiler Council**

Festive Chicken Dip

Deluxe Fajita Nachos

2½ cups shredded, cooked
   chicken
1 package (1.27 ounces)
   LAWRY'S® Spices &
   Seasonings for Fajitas
⅓ cup water
8 ounces tortilla chips
1¼ cups (5 ounces) shredded
   Cheddar cheese

1 cup (4 ounces) shredded
   Monterey Jack cheese
1 large tomato, chopped
1 can (2¼ ounces) sliced
   ripe olives, drained
¼ cup sliced green onions
Salsa

In medium skillet, combine chicken, Spices & Seasonings for Fajitas and water; blend well. Bring to a boil; reduce heat and simmer 3 minutes. In large shallow ovenproof platter, arrange chips. Top with chicken and cheeses. Place under broiler to melt cheese. Top with tomato, olives, green onions and desired amount of salsa.   *Makes 4 appetizer servings*

PRESENTATION: *Serve with guacamole and sour cream.*

SUBSTITUTION: *1¼ pounds cooked ground beef can be used in place of shredded chicken.*

HINT: *For a spicier version, add sliced jalapeños.*

No Way, José Lentil Salsa

2 fresh medium tomatoes
2 cups cooked USA Lentils
1 can (4 ounces) diced
   green chilies
1 cup finely chopped onion
2 tablespoons chopped
   fresh cilantro *or*
   2 teaspoons ground
   coriander

1 tablespoon red wine
   vinegar
1 tablespoon fresh lime
   juice
2 cloves minced garlic
½ teaspoon salt

Chop tomatoes and place in large bowl. Add remaining ingredients and mix well. Chill before serving.
                                          Makes 4 servings

Favorite recipe from **USA Dry Pea & Lentil Council**

Deluxe Fajita Nachos

Layered Guacamole

3 ripe avocados, peeled
  and mashed
1 tablespoon lemon juice
1 package (1.4 ounces)
  onion soup mix
¾ cup DANNON® Plain
  Nonfat or Lowfat
  Yogurt
2 cups shredded Colby-
  Jack cheese (8 ounces)

3 medium tomatoes,
  seeded and diced
¾ cup sliced ripe olives
Salsa
Chopped fresh cilantro
  or parsley
Tortilla chips

In a medium bowl combine avocados and lemon juice. Stir in onion soup mix and yogurt; mix well. Spread avocado mixture onto a round 10- to 12-inch glass serving platter. Top with cheese, tomatoes, olives, salsa and cilantro. Serve with tortilla chips.

Makes 8 servings

Corn Salsa

½ cup WISH-BONE® Italian
  Dressing
1 can (11 ounces) whole
  kernel corn, drained
  (about 1½ cups)
1 medium tomato, diced
  (about 1 cup)
1 medium cucumber,
  peeled, seeded and
  diced (about 1 cup)

¼ cup diced red onion
4 teaspoons finely chopped
  jalapeño pepper or hot
  pepper sauce to taste
  (optional)
1 tablespoon finely
  chopped fresh cilantro
  (optional)
1 teaspoon grated lime
  peel

In medium bowl, thoroughly combine all ingredients. Cover and marinate in refrigerator at least 30 minutes. Serve chilled or at room temperature with your favorite grilled foods.

Makes 10 (⅓-cup) servings

NOTE: *Also terrific with Wish-Bone® Robusto Italian or Lite Italian Dressing.*

Layered Guacamole

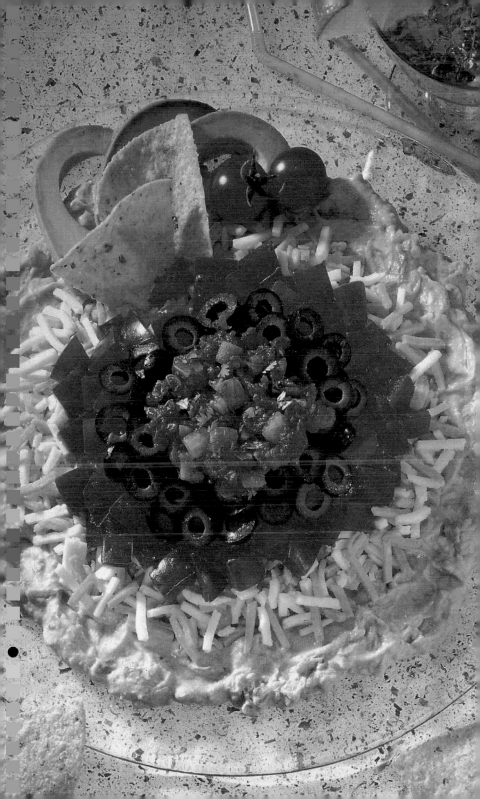

Rio Grande Quesadillas

2 cups shredded, cooked
   chicken
1 package (1.25 ounces)
   LAWRY'S® Taco Spices
   & Seasonings
¾ cup water
1 can (16 ounces) refried
   beans
6 large flour tortillas

1½ cups (6 ounces) shredded
   Monterey Jack cheese
¼ cup chopped pimiento
¼ cup chopped green
   onions
¼ cup chopped fresh
   cilantro
Vegetable oil

In medium skillet, combine chicken, Taco Spices & Seasonings
and water. Bring to a boil; reduce heat and simmer, uncovered,
15 minutes. Stir in refried beans. On half of each tortilla, spread
approximately ⅓ cup of chicken-bean mixture. Layer ⅙ each of
cheese, pimiento, green onions and cilantro on top. Fold each
tortilla in half. In large skillet, heat a small amount of oil and
quickly fry folded tortilla on each side until slightly crisp. Repeat
with each folded tortilla.   *Makes 6 servings*

PRESENTATION: *Cut each quesadilla in quarters and serve with
chunky salsa and guacamole.*

Guacamole

2 avocados, mashed
¼ cup red salsa (mild or
   hot, according to taste)
3 tablespoons NEWMAN'S
   OWN® Salad Dressing

2 tablespoons lime or
   lemon juice
1 clove garlic, finely
   minced
Salt and pepper

Combine all ingredients and mix well. Chill for 1 to 2 hours
tightly covered. Serve with tortilla chips.   *Makes about 2 cups*

Rio Grande Quesadillas

Southwestern Seafood Dip

1 (15-ounce) can pinto
   beans, rinsed and
   drained
1 tablespoon plus
   1 teaspoon taco
   seasoning mix
2 tablespoons fat-free sour
   cream
1 ripe avocado
1 tablespoon lime juice
1 tablespoon fat-free
   mayonnaise
¼ teaspoon Worcestershire
   sauce

⅛ teaspoon chili powder
⅛ teaspoon garlic powder
1 (8-ounce) package surimi
   seafood
3 tablespoons sliced black
   olives
½ small tomato, seeded and
   chopped
¼ cup whole kernel corn
½ cup (2 ounces) shredded
   reduced-fat sharp
   Cheddar cheese
2 tablespoons chopped
   green onion tops

Mash beans with a fork until almost smooth; stir in taco
seasoning mix and sour cream. Spread in an 8-inch circle on a
serving platter; set aside.

Coarsely chop avocado in a bowl; add lime juice, mayonnaise,
Worcestershire sauce, chili powder and garlic powder. Mash with
a fork until mixed well, but not quite smooth. Spread over bean
mixture.

Shred surimi seafood with fingers; sprinkle over avocado layer.
Layer olives, tomato, corn, cheese and onions. Cover and
refrigerate until ready to serve, up to 2 hours. Let stand at room
temperature about 15 minutes before serving. Serve with tortilla
chips.   *Makes about 8 appetizer servings*

Favorite recipe from **Surimi Seafood Education Center**

Southwestern Seafood Dip

Empandillas

½ pound ground beef
1 cup chopped ripe olives
¾ cup chopped fresh
   mushrooms
¼ cup water
1 package (1.25 ounces)
   LAWRY'S® Taco Spices
   & Seasonings

1 package (17¼ ounces)
   frozen puff pastry
   sheets, thawed
1 egg white, beaten

In medium bowl, combine ground beef, olives, mushrooms, water and Taco Spices & Seasonings; blend well. Roll each pastry sheet into a 12-inch square. Cut each sheet into 9 squares. Place approximately 2 teaspoons meat mixture in center of each square; moisten edges with water. Fold one corner over to form triangle and pinch edges together to seal. Brush with egg white. Place on ungreased baking sheet. Bake in 375°F oven 15 to 20 minutes or until golden brown.   *Makes 18 appetizers*

PRESENTATION: *Serve with guacamole and sour cream.*

HINTS: *Two cans (9 ounces each) refrigerated crescent roll dough can be used in place of puff pastry sheets. Roll out dough into two 12-inch squares. Follow directions above. Stir 3 tablespoons grated cheese into the filling for extra flavor.*

South-of-the-Border Sausage Balls

1 pound BOB EVANS
   FARMS® Original
   Recipe Roll Sausage
½ cup dry bread crumbs
¼ cup finely chopped green
   bell pepper
¼ cup finely chopped onion

1 egg, beaten
3 tablespoons chopped
   fresh cilantro
1 tablespoon ground
   cumin
1½ cups chunky salsa

Combine all ingredients except salsa in large bowl until well blended. Shape into 1-inch balls. Cook in large skillet over medium heat until browned on all sides, turning occasionally. Drain off any drippings. Add salsa; bring to a boil over high heat. Reduce heat to low; simmer 10 minutes. Serve hot. Refrigerate leftovers.   *Makes 6 servings*

Independence Day Bean Dip

1 (20.5-ounce) can refried
  beans
1 (16-ounce) jar HUNT'S®
  Homestyle Picante
  Sauce, Mild
1½ cups (6 ounces) shredded
  Cheddar cheese
½ cup sliced black olives
1 (4-ounce) can diced
  green chilies

⅓ cup sliced green onions
¼ cup minced fresh
  cilantro (optional)
¼ teaspoon garlic powder
¼ teaspoon salt
Assorted blue corn and
  yellow corn tortilla
  chips and/or assorted
  fresh raw vegetables in
  season

In large saucepan, combine beans, picante sauce, cheese, olives,
chilies, onions, cilantro, garlic powder and salt. Heat, stirring
frequently, until cheese is melted and beans are heated through.
Serve with chips and vegetables.   *Makes 4¼ cups dip*

Chunky Salsa

2 tablespoons olive oil
1 cup coarsely chopped
  onion
1 cup coarsely diced green
  bell pepper
1 can (35 ounces) tomatoes,
  drained and coarsely
  chopped (reserve
  ½ cup juice)

1 tablespoon freshly
  squeezed lime juice
2 teaspoons TABASCO®
  pepper sauce
½ teaspoon salt
2 tablespoons chopped
  fresh cilantro or
  Italian parsley

Heat oil in a large heavy saucepan over high heat. Add onion and
bell pepper and sauté 5 to 6 minutes, stirring frequently, until
tender. Add tomatoes with reserved ½ cup juice; bring to a boil
over high heat. Reduce heat to low and simmer 6 to 8 minutes,
stirring occasionally, until salsa is slightly thickened. Remove
from heat. Stir in lime juice, Tabasco® sauce to taste and salt.
Cool to lukewarm; stir in cilantro. Spoon salsa into clean jars.
Keep refrigerated for up to 5 days.   *Makes 3½ cups*

Spicy Empanadas

1 can (8¾ ounces)
   garbanzo beans,
   drained
1 teaspoon vegetable oil
¼ cup minced fresh onion
2 tablespoons minced
   green bell pepper
¼ teaspoon LAWRY'S®
   Garlic Powder with
   Parsley
2 tablespoons currants
2 tablespoons chopped
   pitted ripe olives

1 package (1.25 ounces)
   LAWRY'S® Taco Spices
   & Seasonings
1 teaspoon lemon juice
¼ cup (1 ounce) shredded
   Monterey Jack cheese
All-purpose flour
1 sheet frozen puff pastry,
   thawed
1 egg yolk, beaten

Preheat oven to 400°F. In food processor or blender, place garbanzo beans. Pulse 30 seconds to chop finely; set aside. In large skillet, heat oil. Add onion, bell pepper and Garlic Powder with Parsley; sauté 3 to 4 minutes or until vegetables are crisp-tender. Add beans, currants, olives, Taco Spices & Seasonings and lemon juice; cook until mixture thickens, stirring occasionally. Remove from heat; stir in cheese.

On lightly floured surface, roll out pastry sheet to approximately 18 × 10-inch rectangle; cut out six to eight 4-inch circles. Spoon equal amounts of filling onto half of each circle; fold pastry over to form half circle. Press edges together with fork to seal. Place empanadas on greased baking sheet; brush with egg yolk. Bake 18 to 20 minutes or until golden brown. Garnish as desired.

Makes 6 to 8 empanadas

PRESENTATION: *Great with salsa, dairy sour cream and peeled avocado slices.*

HINT: *Double recipe for more appetizers.*

Spicy Empanadas

Spicy Taco Dip

1 pound **BOB EVANS FARMS®** Italian Roll Sausage
1 (13-ounce) can refried beans
1 (8-ounce) jar medium salsa
2 cups (8 ounces) shredded Cheddar cheese
2 cups (8 ounces) shredded Monterey Jack cheese
1 (4-ounce) jar sliced black olives, drained
1 cup sliced green onions with tops
2 cups sour cream
1 (1-pound) bag tortilla chips

Preheat oven to 350°F. Crumble sausage into medium skillet. Cook over medium heat until browned, stirring occasionally. Drain off any drippings. Spread beans in ungreased 2½-quart shallow baking dish, then top with sausage. Pour salsa over sausage; sprinkle with cheeses. Sprinkle olives and onions over top. Bake 20 to 30 minutes or until heated through. Spread with sour cream while hot and serve with chips. Refrigerate leftovers.

Makes 12 to 16 servings

Salsa Italiano

1 pound (2 large) fresh California tomatoes, seeded and diced
½ cup chopped red onion
1 can (2.25 ounces) sliced ripe olives
1 jar (6 ounces) marinated artichoke hearts
2 tablespoons lemon juice
2 garlic cloves, finely chopped
3 tablespoons chopped fresh basil
¼ teaspoon crushed hot red pepper flakes
¼ teaspoon salt
⅛ teaspoon ground black pepper

In a medium bowl, combine tomatoes, onion and olives. Slice artichoke hearts, reserving marinade. Stir artichokes into tomato mixture; set aside. In a small bowl, whisk together lemon juice, garlic, basil, pepper flakes, salt, black pepper and 2 tablespoons artichoke marinade. Gently mix dressing with tomato mixture. Serve with roast or barbecued chicken. *Makes about 2 cups*

Favorite recipe from **California Tomato Board**

Spicy Taco Dip

Fresh Grape Salsa and Chips

¾ cup *each* red and green
    California seedless
    grapes, coarsely
    chopped
½ cup chopped sweet red
    peppers
¼ cup chopped green
    onions
2 tablespoons chopped
    fresh cilantro*

1 tablespoon olive oil
1 tablespoon lime juice
2 teaspoons finely chopped
    jalapeño pepper
½ teaspoon salt
¼ teaspoon bottled hot
    pepper sauce
Tortilla or bagel chips

Combine all ingredients except chips; mix well. Refrigerate for at least 1 hour to allow flavors to blend. Drain well before serving with chips.
    Makes about 1½ cups

*One-fourth cup chopped fresh basil may be substituted.

SERVING TIP: *Serve with cooked fish or chicken, in a roast beef sandwich or on a salad of orange slices.*

Favorite recipe from **California Table Grape Commission**

Mexican Chili Walnuts

2 egg whites, slightly
    beaten
1 tablespoon chili powder
2 teaspoons ground cumin
2 teaspoons salt

1½ teaspoons ground
    cayenne pepper
4 cups (1 pound) walnut
    halves and pieces

Coat a large shallow baking pan with nonstick vegetable spray. Mix egg whites with spices. Stir in walnuts and coat thoroughly. Spread in prepared pan. Bake in 350°F oven 15 to 18 minutes or until dry and crisp. Cool completely before serving.
    Makes 4 cups

NOTE: *Best if made at least one day ahead. Flavors intensify overnight. Store in sealed container.*

Favorite recipe from **Walnut Marketing Board**

Top to bottom: Chili Blanco (page 47) and Fresh Grape Salsa and Chips

Sassy Salads & Sides

◆ ♈ ◆

Border Black Bean Chicken Salad

4 tablespoons olive oil,
  divided
1½ pounds boneless skinless
  chicken breasts, cut
  into 2-inch strips
1 clove garlic, minced
½ jalapeño pepper, seeded
  and finely chopped
1¼ teaspoons salt, divided
4 cups torn romaine
  lettuce
1 can (15 to 16 ounces)
  black beans, drained
  and rinsed

1 cup peeled and seeded
  cucumber cubes
1 cup red bell pepper
  strips
1 cup chopped tomatoes
½ cup chopped red onion
⅓ cup tomato juice cocktail
2 tablespoons fresh lime
  juice
½ teaspoon ground cumin
½ cup chopped pecans,
  toasted*
Fresh parsley for garnish

Heat 2 tablespoons oil in large skillet over medium heat until hot.
Add chicken; stir-fry 2 minutes or until no longer pink in center.
Add garlic, jalapeño and ¾ teaspoon salt; stir-fry 30 seconds.
Combine chicken mixture, lettuce, beans, cucumber, red pepper,
tomatoes and onion in large salad bowl. Combine tomato juice,
lime juice, remaining 2 tablespoons oil, cumin and remaining ½
teaspoon salt in small jar with lid; shake well. Add to skillet; heat
over medium heat until slightly warm. Pour warm dressing over
chicken mixture; toss to coat. Sprinkle with pecans. Garnish with
parsley. Serve immediately.   *Makes 4 servings*

*To toast nuts, place on baking sheet. Bake at 350°F 5 to 7
minutes or until lightly browned.

Favorite recipe from **National Broiler Council**

Border Black Bean Chicken Salad

Acapulco Salad

2 medium navel oranges,
    peeled, sectioned and
    chopped
2 cups peeled and diced
    jicama
1 red bell pepper, diced
1 medium cucumber, diced
½ cup thinly sliced
    radishes
1 large tomato, diced
⅓ cup olive or vegetable oil

3 tablespoons red wine
    vinegar
2 tablespoons lime juice
1 tablespoon chopped
    fresh cilantro
¾ teaspoon LAWRY'S®
    Lemon Pepper
    Seasoning
½ teaspoon LAWRY'S®
    Seasoned Salt

In large bowl, combine oranges and vegetables. In container with stopper or lid, combine remaining ingredients; blend well. Pour over vegetable mixture and toss to coat. Marinate in refrigerator 1 hour before serving. *Makes 4 servings*

PRESENTATION: *Serve this salad alongside your favorite Mexican dishes.*

Arroz Mexicana

1 medium onion, chopped
2 cloves garlic, crushed
½ teaspoon dried oregano,
    crushed
1 tablespoon vegetable oil
¾ cup uncooked long-grain
    white rice

1 can (14½ ounces)
    DEL MONTE® Mexican
    Style Stewed Tomatoes
1 green pepper, chopped

In large skillet, cook onion, garlic and oregano in oil until onion is tender. Stir in rice; cook until rice is golden, stirring frequently. Drain tomatoes reserving liquid; pour liquid into measuring cup. Add water to measure 1½ cups. Stir into rice mixture; bring to boil. Reduce heat; cover and simmer over medium heat 15 minutes or until rice is tender. Stir in tomatoes and green pepper; cook 5 minutes. Garnish with chopped parsley, if desired. *Makes 4 to 6 servings*

Acapulco Salad

South-of-the-Border Vegetable Kabobs

5 cloves garlic, peeled	3 ears corn, cut crosswise
½ cup A.1.® BOLD Steak	into 1½-inch-thick
Sauce	slices and blanched
¼ cup margarine, melted	3 medium plum tomatoes,
1 tablespoon finely	cut into ½-inch slices
chopped fresh cilantro	1 small zucchini, cut
¾ teaspoon ground cumin	lengthwise into thin
¼ teaspoon coarsely	slices
ground black pepper	1 cup baby carrots,
⅛ teaspoon ground red	blanched
pepper	

Mince 1 garlic clove; halve remaining garlic cloves and set aside. In small bowl, combine steak sauce, margarine, cilantro, minced garlic, cumin and peppers; set aside.

Alternately thread vegetables and halved garlic cloves onto 6 (10-inch) metal skewers. Grill kabobs over medium heat for 7 to 9 minutes or until done, turning and basting often with steak sauce mixture. Remove from skewers; serve immediately.

Makes 6 servings

Quick Corn Bread with Chilies 'n' Cheese

1 package (12 to 16 ounces)	1 can (4 ounces) chopped
corn bread or corn	green chilies, drained
muffin mix	1 envelope LIPTON®
1 cup (4 ounces) shredded	Recipe Secrets®
Monterey Jack cheese	Vegetable Soup Mix

Prepare corn bread mix according to package directions; stir in ½ cup cheese, chilies and vegetable soup mix. Pour batter into lightly greased 8-inch baking pan; bake as directed. While warm, top with remaining cheese. Cool completely on wire rack. To serve, cut into squares.

Makes 16 servings

South-of-the-Border Vegetable Kabobs

Aztec Chili Salad

1 pound ground beef
1 package (1.62 ounces)
  LAWRY'S® Spices &
  Seasonings for Chili
½ cup water
1 can (15¼ ounces) kidney
  beans, undrained
1 can (14½ ounces) whole
  peeled tomatoes,
  undrained and cut up
½ cup dairy sour cream
1 fresh medium tomato,
  diced

¼ cup chopped fresh
  cilantro
3 tablespoons mayonnaise
½ teaspoon LAWRY'S®
  Seasoned Pepper
1 head lettuce
1 red bell pepper, sliced
¼ cup sliced green onions
1½ cups (6 ounces) shredded
  Cheddar cheese
¼ cup sliced ripe olives

In large skillet, brown ground beef until cooked; drain fat. Stir in
Spices & Seasonings for Chili, water, beans and canned tomatoes;
blend well. Bring to a boil; reduce heat and simmer, uncovered,
10 minutes. For dressing, in blender or food processor, blend sour
cream, fresh tomato, cilantro, mayonnaise and Seasoned Pepper.
Refrigerate until chilled. On 6 individual plates, layer lettuce,
chili meat, bell pepper, green onions, cheese and olives. Drizzle
with chilled dressing.   *Makes 6 servings*

PRESENTATION: *Serve with jicama wedges arranged around
salad plates.*

HINT: *Ground turkey or shredded chicken can be used in place of
ground beef in chili mixture.*

Aztec Chili Salad

El Dorado Rice Casserole

1 can (14½ ounces) whole peeled tomatoes, cut up	1 teaspoon LAWRY'S® Garlic Salt
1½ cups chicken broth	1 cup dairy sour cream
1 medium onion, chopped	1 can (4 ounces) diced green chilies
1 tablespoon vegetable oil	1½ cups (6 ounces) shredded Monterey Jack cheese
1 cup long-grain rice	

Drain tomatoes, reserving juice. Add reserved juice to broth to make 2½ cups liquid; set aside. In medium saucepan, sauté onion in oil until tender. Add tomato-broth mixture, tomatoes, rice and Garlic Salt. Bring to a boil. Reduce heat; cover and simmer 25 minutes or until liquid is absorbed. In small bowl, combine sour cream and chilies. In 1½-quart casserole, layer ½ of prepared rice, ½ of sour cream mixture and ½ of cheese. Repeat. Bake at 350°F 20 minutes or until bubbly. *Makes 6 servings*

PRESENTATION: *Top casserole with avocado and pimiento slices.*

Black Bean Turkey Pepper Salad

¾ pound fully cooked honey-roasted turkey breast, cut into ¼-inch cubes	1 cup thinly sliced green onions
1 small red bell pepper, cut into ¼-inch cubes	¾ cup chopped fresh cilantro
1 small yellow bell pepper, cut into ¼-inch cubes	2 tablespoons olive oil
1 can (15 ounces) black beans, rinsed and drained	1 tablespoon red wine vinegar
	1 teaspoon ground cumin
	¼ teaspoon cayenne pepper

1. In large bowl combine turkey, red and yellow peppers, black beans, onions and cilantro.

2. In small bowl whisk together oil, vinegar, cumin and cayenne pepper. Fold dressing into turkey mixture. Cover and refrigerate 1 hour. *Makes 6 servings*

Favorite recipe from **National Turkey Federation**

El Dorado Rice Casserole

Gazpacho Salad

1 cup uncooked rice
2½ cups water
½ teaspoon salt
½ cup chunky-style picante
sauce
½ cup tomato juice
1 tablespoon vegetable oil
1 tablespoon garlic red
wine vinegar
½ teaspoon chili powder

1 package (8 ounces)
surimi seafood, broken
into bite-sized pieces
1 cup chopped cucumber
½ cup seeded, chopped
tomato
½ cup chopped green bell
pepper
½ cup sliced cclery
¼ cup sliced green onion

Cook rice with water and salt according to package directions; set aside. Combine picante sauce, tomato juice, oil, vinegar and chili powder in a jar with a tight-fitting lid; cover and shake well. Refrigerate until needed. Combine rice, surimi seafood and remaining ingredients in a large bowl. Add dressing and mix well. Cover and refrigerate at least 2 hours.   *Makes 8 servings*

Favorite recipe from **Surimi Seafood Education Center**

Mexicali Rice and Beans

1 can (14½ ounces) chicken
broth
¾ cup uncooked long-grain
rice
1 can (4 ounces) diced
green chilies, drained
1 package (1.25 ounces)
LAWRY'S® Mexican
Rice Spices &
Seasonings
¾ teaspoon LAWRY'S®
Garlic Powder with
Parsley

½ teaspoon lemon juice
1 can (15 ounces) pinto
beans, drained
1 medium tomato, chopped
1 medium avocado, peeled,
pitted and chopped
1 teaspoon chopped fresh
cilantro

In medium saucepan, combine all ingredients except beans, tomato, avocado and cilantro. Bring to a boil. Reduce heat to low; simmer, uncovered, 20 minutes or until rice is tender, stirring occasionally. Stir in remaining ingredients; simmer 5 minutes.

Makes 4 servings

PRESENTATION: *Serve with soft tacos. Garnish with a sprig of fresh cilantro, if desired.*

Fiesta Corn Casserole

1 tablespoon butter
3 cups corn flakes, divided
1 pound lean ground beef
1 package (1.25 ounces)
    LAWRY'S® Taco Spices
    & Seasonings
½ teaspoon LAWRY'S®
    Seasoned Salt

1 can (8 ounces) tomato
    sauce
1 can (17 ounces) whole
    kernel corn, drained
    (reserve ¼ cup liquid)
2 cups (8 ounces) shredded
    Cheddar cheese

Microwave Directions: In 1½-quart shallow glass casserole, place butter and microwave on HIGH 30 seconds. Sprinkle 2 cups corn flakes over butter. Crush remaining 1 cup corn flakes and set aside. In separate baking dish, microwave ground beef on HIGH 5 minutes, stirring to crumble after 3 minutes. Drain fat and crumble beef. Add Taco Spices & Seasonings, Seasoned Salt, tomato sauce and ¼ cup corn liquid; blend well. Layer half of corn, meat mixture and cheese over buttered corn flakes; repeat layers. Sprinkle remaining 1 cup crushed corn flakes over top in diagonal strips. Microwave on HIGH 12 to 15 minutes.

Makes 4 to 6 servings

PRESENTATION: *Serve with buttered green vegetable, sliced tomatoes and cucumbers, and fresh fruit.*

HINT: *May use 2 cups broken taco shell pieces and 1 cup crushed taco shells.*

South-of-the-Border Salad

2 cups smoked fish, fresh
   or frozen
½ medium head lettuce,
   torn into 2-inch pieces
1 large peeled avocado, cut
   into 1-inch pieces
1 medium tomato, chopped
1 cup diagonally sliced
   celery
1 cup (4 ounces) shredded
   mild Cheddar cheese

½ cup cooked, drained
   garbanzo beans
½ cup chopped green
   onions
½ cup grated carrot
½ cup buttermilk-style
   salad dressing
1 package (4 ounces)
   tortilla chips, lightly
   crushed

Thaw fish if frozen. Break fish into bite-sized pieces. Combine all
ingredients except salad dressing and tortilla chips. Toss well.
Add dressing and tortilla chips and serve immediately.

Makes 6 servings

Favorite recipe from **Florida Department of Agriculture and
Consumer Services**

Upside-Down Corn Bread

1 cup PACE® Picante Sauce
1 cup mixed chopped
   green and red bell
   peppers
1 can (about 8 ounces)
   whole kernel corn,
   drained
2 teaspoons ground cumin

1¼ cups all-purpose flour
¾ cup cornmeal
¼ cup sugar
2 teaspoons baking
   powder
1 cup milk
¼ cup vegetable oil
1 egg, lightly beaten

Combine picante sauce, bell peppers, corn and cumin; mix well.
Spoon evenly onto bottom of lightly greased 11 × 7-inch glass
baking dish. Combine flour, cornmeal, sugar and baking powder.
Add milk, oil and egg, stirring just until dry ingredients are
moistened. Pour evenly over mixture in baking dish. Bake in
preheated 425°F oven 25 minutes or until golden brown. Invert
onto serving platter; let stand 5 minutes. Serve with additional
picante sauce.

Makes 8 servings

South-of-the-Border Salad

Spinach Salad with Orange-Chili Glazed Shrimp

2 teaspoons sesame seeds
¼ cup orange juice
1 tablespoon cider vinegar
1 clove garlic, minced
1 teaspoon grated orange
   peel
1 teaspoon olive oil
½ teaspoon honey
⅛ teaspoon crushed red
   pepper

1 ripe large mango or ripe
   medium papaya
12 cups washed and torn
   fresh spinach leaves
½ cup crumbled feta cheese
   Orange-Chili Glazed
   Shrimp (recipe follows)

Heat small nonstick skillet over medium heat. Add sesame seeds and cook, stirring often, about 4 minutes or until golden. Remove from pan; place in small bowl. Add orange juice, vinegar, garlic, orange peel, oil, honey and red pepper; stir to combine. Set aside.

Peel mango. Cut fruit away from pit; cut into cubes or slices. Discard tough stems from spinach leaves. Place leaves in large bowl and toss with dressing. Top with mango, cheese and shrimp.

Makes 4 servings

Orange-Chili Glazed Shrimp

½ cup orange juice
4 cloves garlic, minced
1 teaspoon chili powder

8 ounces large shrimp,
   peeled, deveined

Combine orange juice, garlic and chili powder in large nonstick skillet. Bring to a boil over high heat. Boil 3 minutes or until mixture just coats bottom of pan. Reduce heat to medium. Add shrimp; cook and stir 2 minutes or until shrimp are opaque and juice mixture coats shrimp. (Add additional orange juice or water to keep shrimp moist, if necessary.)

Makes 4 servings

*Spinach Salad with Orange-Chili
Glazed Shrimp*

Santa Fe Potato Salad

5 medium white potatoes
½ cup vegetable oil
¼ cup red wine vinegar
1 package (1.25 ounces)
LAWRY'S® Taco Spices
& Seasonings
1 can (7 ounces) whole
kernel corn, drained
⅔ cup sliced celery

⅔ cup shredded carrots
⅔ cup chopped red or
green bell pepper
2 cans (2¼ ounces each)
sliced ripe olives,
drained
½ cup chopped red onion
2 tomatoes, wedged and
halved

In large saucepan, cook potatoes in boiling water to cover until tender, about 40 minutes; drain. Cool slightly; cut into cubes. In small bowl, combine oil, vinegar and Taco Spices & Seasonings. Add to warm potatoes and toss gently to coat. Cover; refrigerate at least 1 hour. Gently fold in remaining ingredients. Refrigerate until thoroughly chilled. *Makes 10 servings*

PRESENTATION: *Serve in lettuce-lined bowl with hamburgers or deli sandwiches.*

Fiesta Corn 'n' Peppers

1 medium onion, coarsely
chopped
1 cup mixed diced red and
green bell peppers
1 tablespoon butter or
margarine
1 teaspoon ground cumin
1 can (8¾ ounces) cream-
style corn

1 can (about 8 ounces)
whole kernel corn,
drained, *or* 1 cup
cooked fresh corn
½ cup PACE® Picante Sauce
¼ teaspoon salt
½ cup finely crushed
unsalted tortilla chips
Chopped cilantro
(optional)

Cook and stir onion and peppers in butter in 10-inch skillet until tender, about 4 minutes. Sprinkle with cumin. Stir in cream-style corn, whole kernel corn, picante sauce and salt. Cook until heated through, about 5 minutes, stirring occasionally. Stir in chips; cook and stir until thickened. Sprinkle with cilantro, if desired, and serve with additional picante sauce. *Makes 4 servings*

Santa Fe Potato Salad

Hot Taco Salad

¾ pound lean ground beef (80% lean)
½ cup chopped onion
1 package (6.8 ounces) RICE-A-RONI® Beef Flavor
½ cup salsa
1 teaspoon chili powder

4 cups shredded lettuce
1 medium tomato, chopped
½ cup (2 ounces) shredded Monterey Jack or Cheddar cheese
½ cup crushed tortilla chips (optional)

1. In large skillet, brown ground beef and onion; drain. Remove from skillet; set aside.

2. In same skillet, prepare Rice-A-Roni Mix as package directs.

3. Stir in meat mixture, salsa and chili powder; continue cooking over low heat 3 to 4 minutes or until heated through.

4. Arrange lettuce on serving platter. Top with rice mixture, tomato and cheese. Top with tortilla chips, if desired.

Makes 5 servings

Mexican Pork Salad

1 pound boneless pork loin, cut into 3 × ½ × ¼-inch strips
4 cups shredded lettuce
1 medium orange, peeled, sliced and quartered
1 medium avocado, peeled, seeded and diced

1 small red onion, sliced and separated into rings
1 tablespoon vegetable oil
1 teaspoon chili powder
¾ teaspoon salt
½ teaspoon dried oregano leaves, crushed
¼ teaspoon ground cumin

Place lettuce on serving platter. Arrange orange, avocado and red onion over lettuce. Heat oil in large skillet; add chili powder, salt, oregano and cumin. Add pork loin strips and stir-fry over medium-high heat 5 to 7 minutes or until pork is tender. Spoon hot pork strips over lettuce mixture. Serve immediately.

Makes 4 servings

Favorite recipe from **National Pork Producers Council**

Hot Taco Salad

Soups, Stews & Chilies

◆ 🌵 ◆

Santa Fe Taco Stew

1 tablespoon vegetable oil
½ cup diced onion
½ teaspoon LAWRY'S®
    Garlic Powder with
    Parsley
1 package (1.25 ounces)
    LAWRY'S® Taco Spices
    & Seasonings
1 can (28 ounces) diced
    tomatoes, undrained
1 can (15 ounces) pinto
    beans, drained
1 can (8¾ ounces) whole
    kernel corn, drained

1 can (4 ounces) diced
    green chilies, drained
1 cup beef broth
½ teaspoon cornstarch
1 pound pork butt or beef
    chuck, cooked and
    shredded
Dairy sour cream
    (garnish)
Tortilla chips (garnish)
Fresh cilantro (garnish)

In Dutch oven or large saucepan, heat oil. Add onion and Garlic
Powder with Parsley; sauté 2 to 3 minutes until onion is
translucent and tender. Add Taco Spices & Seasonings, tomatoes,
beans, corn and chilies; blend well. In small bowl, gradually blend
broth into cornstarch using wire whisk. Stir into stew. Stir in
cooked meat. Bring to a boil, stirring frequently. Reduce heat to
low; simmer, uncovered, 30 minutes, stirring occasionally. (Or,
simmer longer for a thicker stew.)   *Makes 8 servings*

PRESENTATION: *Garnish each serving with sour cream, tortilla
chips and fresh cilantro, if desired.*

VARIATION: *Substitute 3 cups cooked, shredded chicken for pork or
beef.*

Taco Twist Soup

1 pound lean ground beef
1 medium onion, chopped
2 cloves garlic, minced
1 to 2 teaspoons chili
   powder
1 teaspoon ground cumin
3 cups beef broth
1½ cups PACE® Picante
   Sauce

1 can (14½ ounces) diced
   tomatoes in juice
1 cup uncooked rotini
   pasta
1 small green pepper,
   chopped
Shredded Cheddar
   cheese
Tortilla chips

In large saucepan, brown ground beef with onion and garlic; drain. Sprinkle chili powder and cumin over meat; cook and stir 30 seconds. Add remaining ingredients except cheese and tortilla chips; mix well. Bring to a boil, stirring frequently. Reduce heat; cover and simmer 10 to 15 minutes or until pasta is tender, stirring occasionally. Serve with cheese, tortilla chips and additional picante sauce. *Makes 8 servings*

Chili Blanco

½ pound diced turkey
   breast (optional)
1 tablespoon vegetable oil
½ cup diced celery
½ cup fresh or canned
   Anaheim chilies
½ cup chopped onion
2 cups water
1 can (16 to 19 ounces)
   small white or red
   kidney beans, drained
1 cup diced fresh tomatoes

1 cup diced zucchini
½ teaspoon salt
½ teaspoon ground cumin
⅛ teaspoon black pepper
⅛ teaspoon ground
   cayenne pepper
Condiments: Shredded
   low fat cheese,
   chopped onion,
   chopped cilantro and
   diced tomatoes
Corn or flour tortillas

Brown turkey in oil in medium saucepan; drain. Add celery, chilies and onion; cook until tender. Add remaining ingredients except condiments and tortillas; mix well. Bring to a boil; reduce heat and simmer 30 minutes. Serve with condiments and tortillas. *Makes 4 servings*

Favorite recipe from **California Table Grape Commission**

Taco Twist Soup

StarKist® Vegetable Gazpacho

1 large onion, quartered
1 medium zucchini, halved
   lengthwise
1 yellow or crookneck
   squash, halved
   lengthwise
1 red bell pepper
1 yellow bell pepper
¾ cup bottled olive oil
   vinaigrette dressing
1 can (6 ounces)
   STARKIST® Solid
   White Tuna, drained
   and chunked

3 pounds firm ripe
   tomatoes, chopped
2 cucumbers, peeled,
   seeded and chopped
2 to 3 cloves fresh garlic,
   minced or pressed
½ cup fresh sourdough
   bread crumbs
1½ to 2 cups tomato juice

Preheat broiler. Brush onion quarters, zucchini halves, squash halves and whole peppers with dressing; reserve remaining dressing. Broil 6 to 8 minutes, turning occasionally, until vegetables are roasted and pepper skins blister and turn black. Remove from broiler. Place peppers in paper bag; close bag and let stand 15 minutes before peeling. Cool remaining vegetables. Peel skin from peppers; seed and remove membranes.

Cut roasted vegetables into large pieces; place in food processor bowl. Process until coarsely chopped. Transfer to large bowl; add tuna, tomatoes, cucumbers, garlic, bread crumbs, 1½ cups tomato juice and remaining dressing. Blend thoroughly. Add remaining ½ cup tomato juice to thin, if necessary. *Makes 6 to 8 servings*

PREP TIME: *30 minutes*

Albóndigas Soup

1 pound ground beef	1 can (14½ ounces) whole
¼ cup long-grain rice	peeled tomatoes,
1 egg	undrained and cut up
1 tablespoon chopped	¼ cup chopped onion
fresh cilantro	1 rib celery, diced
1 teaspoon LAWRY'S®	1 large carrot, diced
Seasoned Salt	1 medium potato, diced
¼ cup ice water	¼ teaspoon LAWRY'S®
2 cans (14½ ounces each)	Garlic Powder with
chicken broth	Parsley

In medium bowl, combine ground beef, rice, egg, cilantro, Seasoned Salt and ice water; form into small meatballs. In large saucepan, combine broth with vegetables and Garlic Powder with Parsley. Bring to a boil; add meatballs. Reduce heat; cover and simmer 30 to 40 minutes, stirring occasionally.

Makes 6 to 8 servings

PRESENTATION: *Serve with lemon wedges and warm tortillas.*

HINT: *For a lower salt version, use homemade chicken broth or low sodium chicken broth.*

Avocado Orange Soup

2 large ripe avocados,	½ teaspoon TABASCO®
pitted	pepper sauce
1 cup fresh orange juice	¼ teaspoon salt
1 cup plain yogurt	Orange slices

In food processor or blender, blend avocados and orange juice. Add yogurt, Tabasco® sauce and salt. Blend until smooth. Refrigerate until ready to serve. Garnish with orange slices.

Makes 4 servings

Albóndigas Soup

Tex-Mex Chicken & Rice Chili

1 package (6.8 ounces)
   RICE-A-RONI® Spanish
   Rice
2¾ cups water
2 cups chopped cooked
   chicken or turkey
1 can (15 or 16 ounces)
   kidney beans or pinto
   beans, rinsed and
   drained
1 can (14½ or 16 ounces)
   tomatoes or stewed
   tomatoes, undrained

1 medium green bell
   pepper, cut into ½-inch
   pieces
1½ teaspoons chili powder
1 teaspoon ground cumin
½ cup (2 ounces) shredded
   Cheddar or Monterey
   Jack cheese (optional)
Sour cream (optional)
Chopped cilantro
   (optional)

1. In 3-quart saucepan, combine rice-vermicelli mix, contents of seasoning packet, water, chicken, beans, tomatoes, green pepper, chili powder and cumin. Bring to a boil over high heat.

2. Reduce heat to low; simmer, uncovered, about 20 minutes or until rice is tender, stirring occasionally.

3. Top with cheese, sour cream and cilantro, if desired.

Makes 4 servings

Salsa Corn Soup with Chicken

3 quarts chicken broth
2 pounds boneless skinless
   chicken breasts,
   cooked and diced
2 (10-ounce) packages
   frozen corn kernels,
   thawed

4 (11-ounce) jars
   NEWMAN'S OWN® All
   Natural Salsa
4 large carrots, cooked and
   diced

Bring chicken broth to a boil in Dutch oven. Add chicken, corn, salsa and carrots. Bring to a boil. Reduce heat and simmer until carrots are tender.

Makes 8 servings

Tex-Mex Chicken & Rice Chili

Nacho Cheese Soup

1 package (about 5 ounces)
   dry au gratin potatoes
1 can (about 15 ounces)
   whole kernel corn,
   undrained
2 cups water
1 cup salsa
2 cups milk

1½ cups (6 ounces)
   SARGENTO® Classic
   Supreme Shredded
   Cheese For Tacos
1 can (about 2 ounces)
   sliced ripe olives,
   drained
Tortilla chips (optional)

In large saucepan, combine potatoes, dry au gratin sauce mix, corn with liquid, water and salsa. Heat to a boil; reduce heat. Cover and simmer 25 minutes or until potatoes are tender, stirring occasionally. Add milk, taco cheese and olives. Cook until cheese is melted and soup is heated through, stirring occasionally. Garnish with tortilla chips. *Makes 6 servings*

Texas Fajita Chili

1¼ cups chopped onions
1 cup chopped green bell
   pepper
1 tablespoon vegetable oil
2 cans (15¼ ounces each)
   kidney beans, drained
1 pound shredded cooked
   pork or beef

1 can (14½ ounces) whole
   peeled tomatoes,
   undrained and cut up
1 cup LAWRY'S® Fajitas
   Skillet Sauce
1 can (7 ounces) whole
   kernel corn, drained
½ cup tomato juice or beer
1½ teaspoons chili powder

In large skillet, sauté onions and bell pepper in oil 10 minutes or until tender. Stir in kidney beans, shredded meat, tomatoes, Fajitas Skillet Sauce, corn, tomato juice and chili powder. Bring mixture to a boil; reduce heat, cover and simmer 20 minutes. *Makes 6 servings*

PRESENTATION: *Serve in individual bowls topped with shredded Monterey Jack cheese or sour cream. If desired, serve with dash of hot pepper sauce.*

Nacho Cheese Soup

30-Minute Chili Olé

1 cup chopped onion
2 cloves garlic, minced
1 tablespoon vegetable oil
2 pounds ground beef
1 (15-ounce) can tomato
    sauce
1 (14½-ounce) can stewed
    tomatoes
¾ cup A.1.® Steak Sauce
1 tablespoon chili powder

1 teaspoon ground cumin
1 (16-ounce) can black
    beans, rinsed and
    drained
1 (11-ounce) can corn,
    drained
Shredded cheese, sour
    cream and chopped
    tomato for garnish

In 6-quart heavy pot, over medium-high heat, sauté onion and garlic in oil until tender. Add beef; cook and stir until browned. Drain; stir in tomato sauce, stewed tomatoes, steak sauce, chili powder and cumin. Heat to a boil; reduce heat to low. Cover; simmer for 10 minutes, stirring occasionally. Stir in beans and corn; simmer, uncovered, for 10 minutes. Serve hot; garnish with cheese, sour cream and tomato.

Makes 8 servings

Baja Corn Chowder

¼ cup butter or margarine
3 cans (17 ounces each)
    whole kernel corn,
    drained, divided
1 medium red bell pepper,
    diced
2 cups chicken broth
1 quart half-and-half
1 can (7 ounces) diced
    green chilies, drained

1 package (1.27 ounces)
    LAWRY'S® Spices &
    Seasonings for Fajitas
2 cups (8 ounces) shredded
    Monterey Jack cheese
½ teaspoon LAWRY'S®
    Seasoned Pepper
Hot pepper sauce to taste

In Dutch oven or large saucepan, melt butter. Add one can of corn and bell pepper; sauté 5 minutes. Remove from heat. In food processor or blender, place remaining two cans of corn and chicken broth; process until smooth. Add to Dutch oven with half-and-half, chilies and Spices & Seasonings for Fajitas. Return to heat. Bring just to a boil, stirring constantly. Remove from heat; blend in cheese, Seasoned Pepper and hot pepper sauce.

Makes 4 to 6 servings

30-Minute Chili Olé

Creamy Gazpacho

1 cup undiluted
  CARNATION®
  Evaporated Skimmed
  Milk
1¾ cups (14.5-ounce can)
  CONTADINA® Recipe
  Ready Diced Tomatoes
2 cups tomato juice
3 tablespoons lemon juice
2 tablespoons olive oil
1 clove garlic, minced
½ teaspoon salt
¼ teaspoon ground black
  pepper

¼ teaspoon red pepper
  sauce
2 cups (2 medium) peeled,
  seeded and diced
  cucumbers
½ cup diced green bell
  pepper
½ cup diced onion
  Garnishes: Plain low fat
  or nonfat yogurt, diced
  cucumber, bell pepper
  and onion (optional)

Place evaporated skimmed milk, tomatoes, tomato juice, lemon juice, olive oil, garlic, salt, pepper and red pepper sauce in blender; cover and blend thoroughly. (Blender container will be very full.)

Pour into serving bowl or tureen and add cucumber, bell pepper and onion; stir thoroughly. Chill. Serve cold; garnish as desired.

Makes about 7 (1-cup) servings

South-of-the-Border Chicken Soup

3 tablespoons vegetable oil
3 corn tortillas cut into
  ½-inch strips
⅓ cup chopped onion
⅔ cup chopped green and
  red peppers
1 clove garlic, minced
¼ cup all-purpose flour

2 (12-ounce) cans chicken
  broth
1 teaspoon chili powder
2 cups cubed cooked
  chicken
1 (16-ounce) can VEG-ALL®
  Mixed Vegetables, with
  liquid

Heat oil in skillet; add tortilla strips and fry, stirring constantly, until golden. Drain on paper towel-lined plate. Add onion and peppers; cook until soft. Add garlic and stir in flour; gradually stir in chicken broth. Add remaining ingredients and heat through. Top with tortilla strips. *Makes 4 to 6 servings*

Creamy Gazpacho

Tacos, Enchiladas & More

◆ 🌵 ◆

Skillet Steak Fajitas

½ cup A.1.® Steak Sauce
½ cup mild, medium or hot thick and chunky salsa
1 (1-pound) beef flank or bottom round steak, thinly sliced
1 medium onion, thinly sliced

1 medium green bell pepper, cut into strips
1 tablespoon margarine
8 (6½-inch) flour tortillas, warmed

Blend steak sauce and salsa. Place steak in glass dish; coat with ¼ cup salsa mixture. Cover; chill 1 hour, stirring occasionally.

In large skillet, over medium-high heat, cook onion and pepper in margarine for 3 minutes or until tender. Remove with slotted spoon; set aside. In same skillet, cook and stir steak for 5 minutes or until done. Add remaining salsa mixture, onion and pepper; cook until heated through. Serve with tortillas and your favorite fajita toppings, if desired. *Makes 4 servings*

Skillet Steak Fajitas

Spicy Bean Tostadas

1 can (15½ ounces) red
   kidney beans, drained
   and rinsed
1 can (14½ ounces) yellow
   hominy, drained
1 can (10 ounces) tomatoes
   with green chilies
1 can (8 ounces) tomato
   sauce
½ cup sliced celery
½ cup chopped onion
1 tablespoon snipped fresh
   parsley
1 teaspoon chili powder
½ teaspoon sugar

1 tablespoon cold water
2 teaspoons cornstarch
4 (6- to 7-inch) corn or
   flour tortillas
2 cups shredded lettuce
2 medium tomatoes,
   chopped
½ cup (2 ounces) shredded
   Cheddar cheese
1 cup DANNON® Plain
   Nonfat or Lowfat
   Yogurt
Taco sauce or salsa
   (optional)

In a large saucepan combine kidney beans, hominy, tomatoes
with green chilies, tomato sauce, celery, onion, parsley, chili
powder and sugar. Bring to a boil; reduce heat. Cover; simmer 10
minutes. Combine cold water and cornstarch; add to saucepan.
Cook and stir until thickened and bubbly; cook and stir 2 minutes
more.

Preheat oven to 350°F. Place tortillas in a single layer on baking
sheet. Bake 10 to 15 minutes or until crisp. Place each tortilla on
a serving plate. Divide bean mixture among tortillas, then
sprinkle with lettuce, tomatoes and cheese. Top with yogurt. If
desired, serve with taco sauce.   *Makes 4 servings*

Spicy Bean Tostada

Border Scramble

1 pound BOB EVANS FARMS® Original Recipe Roll Sausage	½ to 1 tablespoon hot pepper sauce
1½ cups chopped cooked potatoes	½ teaspoon garlic powder
1½ cups chopped onions	½ teaspoon salt
1½ cups chopped tomatoes	4 (9-inch) flour tortillas
¾ cup chopped green bell pepper	2 cups prepared meatless chili
¼ to ½ cup picante sauce	½ cup (2 ounces) shredded Cheddar cheese

Crumble sausage into large skillet. Cook over medium heat until browned, stirring occasionally. Drain off any drippings. Add remaining ingredients except tortillas, chili and cheese; simmer 20 minutes. To warm tortillas, place between paper towels; microwave 1 minute at HIGH. Place 1 cup sausage mixture in center of each tortilla; fold tortilla over filling. Heat chili in small saucepan until hot, stirring occasionally. Top each folded tortilla with ½ cup chili and 2 tablespoons cheese.   *Makes 4 servings*

Chicken Feta Fajitas

1 tablespoon lime juice	1 red pepper, cut into strips
1 teaspoon chili powder	1 package (8 ounces) ATHENOS® Feta Natural Cheese, crumbled
1 teaspoon ground cumin	
3 boneless skinless chicken breast halves (about 1 pound), cut into strips	6 flour tortillas (8 inches), warmed
2 tablespoons vegetable oil	
1 onion, sliced	

• Mix juice, chili powder and cumin in medium bowl. Add chicken; toss lightly.

• Heat oil in large skillet over medium heat. Add chicken mixture; cook and stir 3 minutes. Add onion and pepper; continue cooking 3 minutes or until chicken is cooked through.

• Stir in cheese. Spoon chicken mixture onto tortillas; fold in half.
   Makes 6 servings

Border Scramble

Shrimp Enchiladas

12 ounces cooked shrimp, chopped (2 cups)
1½ cups (6 ounces) shredded Monterey Jack cheese, divided
1¾ cups PACE® Picante Sauce, divided
1½ cups finely chopped fresh broccoli
3 ounces cream cheese, softened
½ cup thinly sliced green onions with tops
⅓ cup chopped fresh cilantro
½ teaspoon garlic salt
Vegetable oil
12 corn tortillas*
Optional toppings: chopped tomato, avocado slices, sour cream

Combine shrimp, ½ cup shredded cheese, ½ cup picante sauce, broccoli, cream cheese, onions, cilantro and garlic salt; mix well. Heat about ½ inch of oil in small skillet until hot. Quickly fry each tortilla in oil to soften, about 2 seconds per side; drain on paper towels. Spoon ⅓ cup shrimp mixture down center of each tortilla; roll up and place seam side down in 13 × 9-inch baking dish. Spoon remaining 1¼ cups picante sauce evenly over enchiladas. Bake, uncovered, at 350°F 25 minutes. Sprinkle with remaining 1 cup cheese. Return to oven until cheese melts. Serve with toppings and additional picante sauce.   *Makes 6 servings*

*Flour tortillas may be substituted; omit frying.

Tuna Salad Burritos

2 cans (6½ ounces each) or 1 can (13 ounces) solid white tuna in water, drained and flaked
½ cup sliced ripe olives
½ cup sliced green onions with tops
½ cup thinly sliced celery
⅔ cup PACE® Picante Sauce
½ cup nonfat or light dairy sour cream
1 teaspoon ground cumin
12 taco shells
12 small lettuce leaves

Combine tuna, olives, green onions and celery in medium bowl; set aside. Combine picante sauce, sour cream and cumin; mix well. Pour over tuna mixture and toss lightly. To serve, line taco shells with lettuce leaf; spoon tuna mixture into shells. Serve with additional picante sauce.   *Makes 12 servings*

Shrimp Enchiladas

Tuna Fiesta Soft Tacos

⅓ cup mayonnaise
½ teaspoon garlic salt
½ teaspoon lemon pepper
  seasoning
1 can (6 ounces)
  STARKIST® Solid
  White or Chunk Light
  Tuna, drained and
  flaked
¼ cup chopped celery
1 hard-cooked egg,
  chopped
2 tablespoons finely
  chopped green onion

2 tablespoons finely
  chopped green bell
  pepper
1 tablespoon drained
  chopped pimiento
6 flour tortillas (6 inches
  each), warmed
1 cup shredded iceberg
  lettuce
½ cup shredded Colby or
  Monterey Jack cheese
Salsa (optional)

In large bowl, combine mayonnaise, garlic salt, lemon pepper seasoning, tuna, celery, egg, onion, bell pepper and pimiento; mix thoroughly. Place generous ¼ cup filling on one side of each tortilla; top with lettuce and cheese. Fold tortilla over; serve with salsa, if desired. *Makes 6 servings*

Breakfast Quesadillas

1 pound BOB EVANS
  FARMS® Original
  Recipe Roll Sausage
4 eggs
4 (10-inch) flour tortillas

2 cups (8 ounces) shredded
  Monterey Jack cheese
½ cup chopped green
  onions with tops
½ cup chopped tomato
  Sour cream and salsa

Crumble sausage into large skillet. Cook over medium heat until sausage is browned, stirring occasionally. Drain off any drippings. Remove sausage to paper towels; set aside. Add eggs to same skillet; scramble until eggs are set but not dry. Remove eggs; set aside. Place 1 tortilla in same skillet. Top with half of each eggs, cheese, sausage, onions and tomato. Heat until cheese melts; top with another tortilla. Remove from skillet; cut into six equal wedges. Repeat with remaining tortillas, eggs, cheese, sausage, onions and tomato to make second quesadilla. Serve hot with sour cream and salsa. Refrigerate leftovers. *Makes 4 servings*

Tuna Fiesta Soft Taco

Huevos Rancheros Tostados

1 can (8 ounces) tomato
    sauce
⅓ cup prepared salsa or
    picante sauce
¼ cup chopped fresh
    cilantro or thinly
    sliced green onions
4 large eggs

Butter or margarine
4 corn tortillas (6 inches),
    crisply fried *or* 4
    prepared tostada shells
1 cup (4 ounces)
    SARGENTO® Shredded
    Cheese For Tacos

Combine tomato sauce, salsa and cilantro; heat in microwave oven or in saucepan over medium-high heat until hot. Fry eggs in butter, sunny side up. Place one egg on each tortilla; top with sauce. Sprinkle with taco cheese. *Makes 4 servings*

VARIATION: *Spread tortillas with heated refried beans before topping with eggs, if desired.*

Tacos

1 pound BOB EVANS
    FARMS® Original
    Recipe or Zesty Hot
    Roll Sausage
1 (8-ounce) jar taco sauce
1 package taco shells (10 to
    12 count)
2 cups (8 ounces) shredded
    Cheddar cheese

1 large onion, chopped
2 tomatoes, chopped
¼ head iceberg lettuce,
    shredded
Fresh cilantro sprigs and
    bell pepper triangles
    (optional)

Preheat oven to 350°F. Crumble sausage into medium skillet; cook over medium-high heat until browned, stirring occasionally. Drain off any drippings. Stir in taco sauce. Bring to a boil. Reduce heat to low; simmer 5 minutes. Meanwhile, bake taco shells until warm and crisp. To assemble tacos, place 2 tablespoons sausage mixture in each taco shell and top evenly with cheese, onion, tomatoes and lettuce. Garnish with cilantro and pepper triangles, if desired. Serve hot. Refrigerate any leftover filling. *Makes 10 to 12 servings*

Huevos Rancheros Tostado

Rice & Bean Burritos

FILLING

1 tablespoon olive or
    vegetable oil
½ cup sliced green onions
1 jalapeño pepper, seeded
    and chopped
2 to 3 cloves garlic, minced
½ pound lean ground beef,
    turkey or chicken

2 cups water
1 can (14½ ounces)
    chopped tomatoes,
    undrained
1 package (8 ounces)
    FARMHOUSE®
    Mexican Beans & Rice
Salt and pepper

BURRITO FIXINGS

6 large *or* 12 small flour
    tortillas, softened
    Shredded Cheddar
    cheese

Sour cream
Prepared salsa

For filling, in large skillet, heat oil until hot. Cook and stir onions,
jalapeño and garlic in hot oil until garlic is tender but not brown.
Add ground meat; cook until meat is no longer pink. Add water
and undrained tomatoes; bring to a boil. Add beans & rice and
contents of seasoning packet. Reduce heat; cover and simmer 25
minutes. Season to taste with salt and pepper.

To assemble burritos, place ⅔ cup meat mixture in center of large
tortilla (⅓ cup for small tortillas). Top with shredded cheese, sour
cream and salsa. Fold up burrito style and serve immediately.

Makes 6 servings

Red Chili Tortilla Torte

2 cans (16 ounces) pinto
    beans or black beans,
    rinsed and drained
¼ cup low-salt chicken
    broth
1 tablespoon vegetable oil
2 large onions, sliced
2 red bell peppers, cut into
    ¼-inch strips
2 zucchini, thinly sliced

2 cloves garlic, minced
1 cup whole kernel corn
1 teaspoon ground cumin
½ teaspoon salt
¼ teaspoon cayenne pepper
6 (8-inch) flour tortillas
2 cups NEWMAN'S OWN®
    All Natural Salsa
2 cups (8 ounces) shredded
    Monterey Jack cheese

In food processor, combine pinto beans and chicken broth. Process until smooth; set aside. Heat oil in large nonstick skillet over medium heat. Add onions, bell peppers, zucchini and garlic; sauté until softened, 10 to 12 minutes. Add corn, cumin, salt and cayenne pepper; cook about 2 minutes.

Heat oven to 375°F. Grease 8 inch round baking dish. Spread ½ cup of pinto bean mixture on one flour tortilla; place on bottom of baking dish. Spoon 1 cup of the onion mixture on top of the beans. Spoon ⅓ cup of Newman's Own® All Natural Salsa on top of onion mixture; top with ⅓ cup of cheese. Repeat with remaining ingredients, ending with cheese. Bake until heated through, about 45 minutes. Let stand 10 minutes; cut into wedges to serve.   *Makes 8 to 10 servings*

Enchiladas Fantasticas

1 pound ground turkey
2 cups PACE® Picante
    Sauce, divided
1 package (10 ounces)
    frozen chopped
    spinach, thawed,
    squeezed dry
2 teaspoons ground cumin,
    divided
½ teaspoon salt
1 package (8 ounces)
    regular or light cream
    cheese, cubed

12 flour tortillas (7 inches),
    warmed
1 can (14½ ounces) diced
    tomatoes, undrained
1 cup (4 ounces) shredded
    Cheddar cheese
Optional toppings:
    shredded lettuce, ripe
    olive slices, avocado
    slices, sour cream

In 10-inch nonstick skillet, cook turkey until no longer pink, breaking into small pieces with spoon. Add 1 cup picante sauce, spinach, 1½ teaspoons cumin and salt. Cook and stir 5 minutes or until most of the liquid has evaporated. Add cream cheese, stirring just until melted; remove from heat. Spoon about ⅓ cup filling down center of each tortilla; roll up and place seam side down in lightly greased 13 × 9-inch baking dish. Combine tomatoes, remaining 1 cup picante sauce and remaining ½ teaspoon cumin; mix well. Spoon over enchiladas. Bake at 350°F 20 minutes or until hot. Sprinkle with Cheddar cheese; return to oven 2 minutes to melt cheese. Top as desired and serve with additional picante sauce.   *Makes 6 servings*

Baja Beef Enchiladas

1 pound lean ground beef
1 medium onion, chopped
2 cloves garlic, minced
1 can (16 ounces) whole tomatoes, drained and coarsely chopped
1 package (10 ounces) frozen chopped spinach, thawed, squeezed dry and finely chopped
1¾ cups PACE® Picante Sauce, divided

1½ teaspoons ground cumin
½ teaspoon salt
2 cups (8 ounces) shredded Monterey Jack or Cheddar cheese, divided
Vegetable oil
12 corn tortillas
Optional toppings: sliced ripe olives, avocado slices, sour cream, chopped tomatoes

Brown meat with onion and garlic in 10-inch skillet; drain. Add tomatoes, spinach, ½ cup picante sauce, cumin and salt. Bring to a boil. Reduce heat; cover and simmer 5 minutes. Stir in 1 cup cheese. Heat about ½ inch of oil in small skillet until hot. Quickly fry each tortilla in oil to soften, about 2 seconds per side; drain on paper towels. Spoon about ⅓ cup mixture down center of each tortilla; roll up and place seam side down in ungreased 13 × 9-inch baking dish. Spoon remaining 1¼ cups picante sauce evenly over tortillas. Bake uncovered at 350°F 15 minutes or until hot. Sprinkle with remaining 1 cup cheese. Return to oven until cheese melts. Top as desired and serve with additional picante sauce. *Makes 6 servings*

Baja Beef Enchiladas

Bean and Vegetable Burritos

1 tablespoon olive oil
1 medium onion, thinly
 sliced
1 jalapeño pepper, seeded,
 minced
1 tablespoon chili powder
3 cloves garlic, minced
2 teaspoons dried oregano
 leaves, crushed
1 teaspoon ground cumin
1 large sweet potato,
 baked, cooled, peeled,
 diced *or* 1 can
 (16 ounces) yams in
 syrup, drained, rinsed,
 diced

1 can black beans or pinto
 beans, drained, rinsed
1 cup frozen whole kernel
 corn, thawed, drained
1 green bell pepper,
 chopped
2 tablespoons lime juice
¾ cup (3 ounces) shredded
 reduced fat Monterey
 Jack cheese
4 (10-inch) flour tortillas
 Low fat sour cream
 (optional)

Preheat oven to 350°F. Heat oil in large saucepan or Dutch oven over medium-high heat. Add onion and cook, stirring often, 10 minutes or until golden. Add jalapeño, chili powder, garlic, oregano and cumin; stir 1 minute. Add 1 tablespoon water and stir; remove from heat. Stir in sweet potato, beans, corn, green pepper and lime juice.

Spoon 2 tablespoons cheese in center of each tortilla. Top with 1 cup filling. Fold all 4 sides around filling to enclose. Place burritos seam side down on baking sheet. Cover with foil and bake 30 minutes or until heated through. Serve with sour cream, if desired. *Makes 4 servings*

Bean and Vegetable Burrito

Tex-Mex Chicken Fajitas

6 boneless skinless chicken
  breast halves (about
  1½ pounds), cut into
  strips
½ cup LAWRY'S® Mesquite
  Marinade with Lime
  Juice*
3 tablespoons plus
  1½ teaspoons vegetable
  oil, divided
1 small onion, sliced and
  separated into rings
1 medium-sized green bell
  pepper, cut into strips

¾ teaspoon LAWRY'S®
  Garlic Powder with
  Parsley
½ teaspoon hot pepper
  sauce
1 medium tomato, cut into
  wedges
2 tablespoons chopped
  fresh cilantro
Flour tortillas, warmed
1 medium lime, cut into
  wedges

Pierce chicken several times with fork; place in large resealable
plastic bag or bowl. Pour Mesquite Marinade with Lime Juice
over chicken; seal bag or cover bowl. Refrigerate at least 30
minutes. Heat 1 tablespoon plus 1½ teaspoons oil in large skillet.
Add onion, bell pepper, Garlic Powder with Parsley and hot
pepper sauce; sauté 5 to 7 minutes or until onion is crisp-tender.
Remove vegetable mixture from skillet; set aside. Heat remaining
2 tablespoons oil in same skillet. Add chicken; sauté 8 to 10
minutes or until chicken is no longer pink in center, stirring
frequently. Return vegetable mixture to skillet with tomato and
cilantro; heat through.   *Makes 4 to 6 servings*

PRESENTATION: *Serve with flour tortillas and lime wedges. Top
with dairy sour cream, guacamole, salsa and pitted ripe olives as
desired.*

*One package (1.27 ounces) Lawry's® Spices & Seasonings for
Fajitas, ¼ cup lime juice and ¼ cup vegetable oil can be
substituted.

Tex-Mex Chicken Fajitas

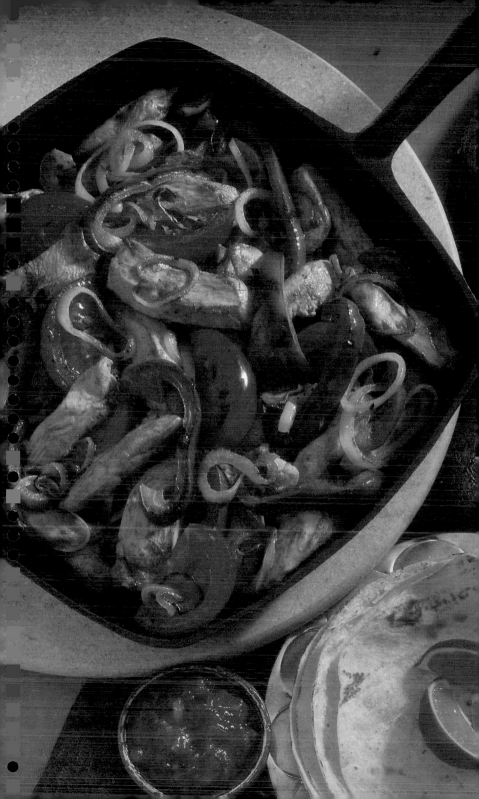

Tacos Picadillos

¾ **pound ground pork**
1 medium onion, chopped
½ **teaspoon ground**
   cinnamon
½ **teaspoon ground cumin**
1 can (14½ ounces)
   DEL MONTE® Mexican
   Style Stewed Tomatoes

⅓ **cup DEL MONTE®**
   Seedless Raisins
⅓ **cup toasted chopped**
   almonds
6 flour tortillas

In large skillet, brown meat with onion and spices over medium-high heat. Season to taste with salt and pepper, if desired. Stir in tomatoes and raisins. Cover and cook 10 minutes. Remove cover; cook over medium-high heat 5 minutes or until thickened, stirring occasionally. Just before serving, stir in almonds. Fill tortillas with meat mixture; roll to enclose. Garnish with lettuce, cilantro and sour cream, if desired. Serve immediately.

Makes 6 servings

HELPFUL HINT: *If ground pork is not available, boneless pork may be purchased and ground in food processor. Cut pork into 1-inch cubes before processing.*

Fantastic Pork Fajitas

1 pound pork strips
2 teaspoons vegetable oil
½ **medium onion, peeled**
   and sliced

1 green pepper, seeded and
   sliced
4 flour tortillas, warmed

Heat large nonstick skillet over medium-high heat. Add oil; heat until hot. Add pork strips, onion and pepper slices to skillet and stir-fry quickly 4 to 5 minutes. Roll up portions of the meat mixture in flour tortillas and serve with purchased salsa, if desired.

Makes 4 servings

Favorite recipe from **National Pork Producers Council**

Tacos Picadillos

Enchiladas de Puerco y Frijoles

¾ **pound lean ground pork**
   or beef
2 **cloves garlic, minced**
1½ **cups PACE® Picante**
   Sauce, divided
1 **can (16 ounces) black**
   beans or pinto beans,
   rinsed and drained
1 **can (8 ounces)**
   tomatoes, drained
1 **can (8 ounces) whole**
   kernel corn, drained

2 **teaspoons ground cumin**
1 **teaspoon chili powder**
⅓ **cup thinly sliced green**
   onions with tops
12 **flour tortillas**
   (6 to 7 inches)
1 **cup (4 ounces) shredded**
   Cheddar cheese
Toppings: sour cream,
   chopped cilantro

Brown meat with garlic in 10-inch skillet; drain. Add ½ cup picante sauce, beans, tomatoes, corn and seasonings; mix well. Cook, stirring frequently, 5 minutes or until most of liquid has evaporated. Stir in green onions. Spoon about ⅓ cup meat mixture down center of each tortilla; roll up. Place seam side down in 13 × 9-inch baking dish. Spoon remaining 1 cup picante sauce evenly over enchiladas. Bake at 350°F 15 minutes or until hot. Top with cheese; return to oven 3 minutes or until cheese melts. Top as desired and serve with additional picante sauce.

Makes 6 servings

Special Beef and Spinach Burritos

1 **pound lean ground beef**
1 **small onion, chopped**
1 **clove garlic, crushed**
½ **teaspoon salt**
½ **teaspoon chili powder**
¼ **teaspoon ground cumin**
¼ **teaspoon black pepper**
1 **package (10 ounces)**
   frozen chopped
   spinach, thawed, well
   drained
2 **jalapeño peppers,**
   seeded, finely chopped

1½ **cups shredded Monterey**
   Jack cheese
4 **large (10-inch)** *or*
   8 **medium (8-inch) flour**
   tortillas, warmed
Lime slices (optional)
Jalapeño pepper slices
   (optional)
1 **cup prepared chunky**
   salsa

In large nonstick skillet, brown beef, onion and garlic over medium heat 8 to 10 minutes or until beef is no longer pink, stirring occasionally. Pour off drippings. Season with salt, chili powder, cumin and black pepper. Stir in spinach and jalapeño peppers; heat through. Remove from heat; stir in cheese.

To serve, spoon equal amount of beef mixture into center of each tortilla. Fold bottom edge up over filling. Fold right and left sides to center, overlapping edges. Garnish with lime and jalapeño slices, if desired. Serve with salsa. *Makes 4 servings*

Favorite recipe from **North Dakota Beef Commission**

Quick 'n' Easy Tacos

1 pound ground beef
1 can (14½ ounces) whole peeled tomatoes, undrained and coarsely chopped
1 medium green bell pepper, finely chopped

1 envelope LIPTON® Recipe Secrets® Onion Soup Mix
1 tablespoon chili powder
3 drops hot pepper sauce (optional)
8 taco shells
Taco Toppings

In medium skillet, brown ground beef over medium-high heat; drain. Stir in tomatoes, green pepper, onion soup mix, chili powder and hot pepper sauce. Bring to a boil, then simmer 15 minutes or until slightly thickened. Serve in taco shells with assorted Taco Toppings. *Makes 4 servings*

TACO TOPPINGS: *Use shredded Cheddar or Monterey Jack cheese, shredded lettuce, chopped tomatoes, sliced pitted ripe olives, sour cream or taco sauce.*

NOTE: *Also terrific with Lipton® Recipe Secrets® Onion-Mushroom or Beefy Mushroom Soup Mix.*

Breakfast Burritos with Baked Citrus Fruit

4 green onions, thinly sliced, divided
1¼ cups frozen egg substitute, thawed
2 tablespoons diced mild green chilies
½ cup (2 ounces) shredded reduced fat Monterey Jack or Cheddar cheese

¼ cup lightly packed fresh cilantro
4 (7-inch) flour tortillas
¼ cup salsa
¼ cup low fat sour cream
Baked Citrus Fruit (recipe follows)

Spray large nonstick skillet with cooking spray. Heat over medium heat. Set aside ¼ cup green onions. Add remaining onions, egg substitute and chilies. Cook, stirring occasionally, about 4 minutes or until eggs are softly set. Stir in cheese and cilantro. Continue cooking, folding eggs over until eggs are cooked to desired doneness, about 1 minute.

Stack tortillas and wrap in paper towels. Microwave at HIGH about 1 minute or until hot. Place one-quarter of eggs in center of each tortilla. Fold sides over filling to enclose. Place burritos seam side down on plates. Top each with salsa, 1 tablespoon sour cream and reserved green onions. Serve with Baked Citrus Fruit.

Makes 4 servings

Baked Citrus Fruit

2 oranges, peeled and sliced
1 grapefruit, peeled and sliced

1½ tablespoons lightly packed brown sugar
½ teaspoon ground cinnamon

Preheat oven to 400°F. Divide fruit slices into 4 portions. Arrange each portion on baking sheet, overlapping slices. Combine brown sugar and cinnamon in small bowl. Sprinkle 1 teaspoon brown sugar mixture over each serving of fruit. Bake 5 minutes or until fruit is hot.

Makes 4 servings

Breakfast Burritos with Baked Citrus Fruit

Ensenada Fish Tacos

10 ounces halibut or orange
  roughy fillets, cut into
  1-inch cubes
1 tablespoon vegetable oil
1 tablespoon lime juice
1 package (1.27 ounces)
  LAWRY'S® Spices &
  Seasonings for Fajitas
6 corn or flour tortillas
  (about 8 inches)
2½ cups shredded lettuce
½ cup diced tomatoes

¾ cup (3 ounces) shredded
  Monterey Jack or
  Cheddar cheese
2 tablespoons thinly sliced
  green onion
Dairy sour cream
  (garnish)
Guacamole (garnish)
Salsa (garnish)
Chopped fresh cilantro
  (garnish)

In shallow glass baking dish, place fish. Pour oil and lime juice over fish. Sprinkle with Spices & Seasonings for Fajitas; toss lightly to coat. Cover. Refrigerate 2 hours to marinate, occasionally spooning marinade over fish. In same dish, bake fish in 450°F oven 10 minutes or until fish flakes easily with fork; drain. To serve, evenly divide fish; place in center of each tortilla. Top with lettuce, tomatoes, cheese and green onion.

Makes 6 servings

Turkey Tacos

1 pound ground turkey
2 tablespoons minced
  dried onion
1 tablespoon chili powder
1 teaspoon paprika
½ teaspoon *each* cumin,
  dried oregano and salt
¼ teaspoon garlic powder

⅛ teaspoon black pepper
10 taco shells
1 to 2 tomatoes, chopped
2 to 3 cups shredded
  lettuce
⅔ cup shredded reduced-
  fat Cheddar cheese

In large nonstick skillet over medium-high heat, cook and stir turkey, onion and seasonings 5 to 6 minutes or until turkey is no longer pink. Spoon mixture evenly into taco shells and top with tomatoes, lettuce and cheese.

Makes 5 servings

Favorite recipe from **National Turkey Federation**

Ensenada Fish Tacos

Spicy Burrito Burgers

6 tablespoons prepared
mild salsa, divided
1 can (4 ounces) diced
green chilies, divided
¼ cup sour cream
Dash hot pepper sauce

1 pound ground beef
4 (6-inch) flour tortillas
1 cup shredded lettuce
½ cup (2 ounces) shredded
Cheddar cheese with
taco seasonings

Combine 2 tablespoons salsa, 2 tablespoons chilies, sour cream
and hot pepper sauce in small bowl; set aside.

Combine beef, remaining 4 tablespoons salsa and remaining
chilies in large bowl; mix well. Shape into four 4-inch oval patties.

Grill burgers over medium coals 8 to 10 minutes for medium or
until desired doneness is reached, turning halfway through
grilling time.

Place 1 burger in center of 1 tortilla. Top with one-quarter of the
lettuce, cheese and sour cream mixture. Bring edges of tortilla
together over top of burger; secure with toothpick if necessary.
Remove toothpick before serving.   *Makes 4 servings*

Breakfast Tacos

½ cup chopped green
pepper
½ cup chopped onion
2 tablespoons butter or
margarine
6 eggs, lightly beaten
¾ cup PACE® Picante
Sauce, divided

½ teaspoon garlic salt
½ teaspoon ground cumin
1½ cups (6 ounces) shredded
Monterey Jack or
Cheddar cheese,
divided
8 taco shells, heated
8 avocado slices (optional)

Cook pepper and onion in butter in 10-inch skillet until tender
but not brown. Stir in eggs, ¼ cup picante sauce, garlic salt and
cumin. Cook over medium-low heat, stirring frequently, until eggs
are set. Remove from heat; stir in 1 cup cheese. Fill taco shells
with egg mixture. Top each with avocado, if desired, 1 tablespoon
of remaining cheese and 1 tablespoon of remaining picante sauce.
Makes 4 servings

Spicy Burrito Burger

Mexican Main Dishes
◆ 🌵 ◆

Classic Arroz con Pollo

2 tablespoons olive oil
1 broiler-fryer chicken
(about 2 pounds),
cut up
2 cups uncooked long-
grain rice
1 cup chopped onion
1 medium-size red bell
pepper, chopped
1 medium-size green bell
pepper, chopped
1 clove garlic, minced
1½ teaspoons salt, divided

1½ teaspoons dried basil
4 cups chicken broth
1 tablespoon lime juice
⅛ teaspoon ground saffron
or ½ teaspoon ground
turmeric
1 bay leaf
2 cups chopped tomatoes
½ teaspoon ground black
pepper
1 cup fresh or frozen green
peas
Fresh basil for garnish

Heat oil in Dutch oven over medium-high heat until hot. Add
chicken; cook 10 minutes or until browned, turning occasionally.
Remove chicken; keep warm. Add rice, onion, red pepper, green
pepper, garlic, ¾ teaspoon salt and basil to Dutch oven; cook and
stir 5 minutes or until vegetables are tender and rice is browned.
Add broth, lime juice, saffron and bay leaf. Bring to a boil; stir in
tomatoes. Arrange chicken on top and sprinkle with remaining
¾ teaspoon salt and black pepper. Cover; reduce heat to low. Cook
20 minutes more. Stir in peas; cover and cook 10 minutes more or
until fork can be inserted into chicken with ease and juices run
clear, not pink. Remove bay leaf. Garnish with basil. Serve
immediately. *Makes 8 servings*

Favorite recipe from **USA Rice Council**

Classic Arroz con Pollo

Chili Pizza

1 can (15 ounces) kidney
   beans, rinsed and
   drained
3 slices bacon, diced
½ pound ground beef chuck
2 cups PACE® Picante
   Sauce
1 teaspoon ground cumin

1 (12-inch) prebaked pizza
   crust or Italian bread
   shell
2 cups (8 ounces) shredded
   Cheddar cheese
1 cup mixed short, thin red
   and green bell pepper
   strips

Partially mash kidney beans with fork. Cook bacon in 10-inch skillet until crisp; remove to paper towels with slotted spoon. Wipe out skillet with paper towel. In same skillet, brown ground beef; drain. Add picante sauce, beans and cumin; bring to a boil. Reduce heat and simmer uncovered, stirring frequently, 10 to 12 minutes or until mixture is thickened. Place pizza crust on pizza pan or cookie sheet; spoon meat mixture onto crust. Sprinkle with bacon and half the cheese. Top evenly with peppers; sprinkle with remaining cheese. Bake at 350°F 20 minutes. Cut into wedges and serve with additional picante sauce.   *Makes 4 servings*

Tijuana Blackened Steak

¾ teaspoon garlic powder
¾ teaspoon onion powder
¾ teaspoon ground black
   pepper
½ teaspoon ground white
   pepper
¼ teaspoon ground red
   pepper

4 (4- to 6-ounce) beef shell
   or strip steaks, about
   ½ inch thick
½ cup A.1.® Steak Sauce
¼ cup margarine, melted

In small bowl, combine garlic powder, onion powder and peppers; spread on waxed paper. Coat both sides of steaks with seasoning mixture.

In small bowl, combine steak sauce and margarine; set aside ½ cup. Grill steaks 10 to 15 minutes or until done, turning and brushing often with ¼ cup steak sauce mixture. Serve steaks with reserved ½ cup steak sauce mixture.   *Makes 4 servings*

Chili Pizza

Mexicali Beef & Rice

1 package (6.8 ounces)
  RICE-A-RONI® Beef
  Flavor
1 cup frozen corn *or* 1 can
  (8 ounces) whole
  kernel corn, drained
½ cup chopped red or
  green bell pepper

1 pound lean ground beef
  (80% lean)
Salt and pepper
  (optional)
Salsa (optional)
Sour cream (optional)

1. Prepare Rice-A-Roni Mix as package directs, stirring in frozen corn and red pepper during last 10 minutes of cooking.

2. While Rice-A-Roni is simmering, shape beef into four ½-inch-thick patties.

3. In lightly greased second large skillet, cook beef patties over medium heat, about 4 minutes on each side or until desired doneness. Season with salt and pepper, if desired.

4. Serve rice topped with cooked beef patties, salsa and sour cream, if desired.   *Makes 4 servings*

Pork Tenderloin Mole

1½ pounds pork tenderloin
  (about 2 whole)
1 teaspoon vegetable oil
½ cup chopped onion
1 clove garlic, minced
1 cup Mexican-style chili
  beans, undrained
¼ cup chili sauce

¼ cup raisins
2 tablespoons water
1 tablespoon peanut butter
1 teaspoon unsweetened
  cocoa
Dash *each* salt, ground
  cinnamon and ground
  cloves

Place tenderloin in shallow baking pan. Roast at 350°F for 30 minutes or until juicy and slightly pink in center.

Heat oil in medium saucepan. Cook onion and garlic over low heat for 5 minutes. Combine onion and garlic with remaining ingredients in food processor; mix until almost smooth. Heat mixture in saucepan thoroughly over low temperature, stirring frequently. Serve over tenderloin slices.   *Makes 6 servings*

Favorite recipe from **National Pork Producers Council**

Mexicali Beef & Rice

Spicy Tuna Empanadas

1 can (6 ounces) STARKIST® Solid White or Chunk Light Tuna, drained and flaked	Salt and pepper to taste
	¼ teaspoon hot pepper sauce
1 can (4 ounces) diced green chilies, drained	¼ cup medium thick and chunky salsa
1 can (2¼ ounces) sliced ripe olives, drained	2 packages (15 ounces each) refrigerated pie crusts
½ cup shredded sharp Cheddar cheese	Additional salsa
1 chopped hard-cooked egg	

In medium bowl, place tuna, chilies, olives, cheese, egg, salt, pepper and hot pepper sauce; toss lightly with fork. Add ¼ cup salsa and toss again; set aside. Following directions on package, unfold crusts (roll out slightly with rolling pin if you prefer thinner crust); cut 4 circles, 4 inches *each,* out of each crust. Place 8 circles on foil-covered baking sheets; wet edge of each circle with water. Top each circle with ¼ cup lightly packed tuna mixture. Top with remaining circles, stretching pastry slightly to fit; press edges together and crimp with fork. Cut slits in top crust to vent. Bake in 425°F oven 15 to 18 minutes or until golden brown. Cool slightly. Serve with additional salsa. *Makes 8 servings*

Burgers Olé!

1½ pounds lean ground beef	1 egg
1 cup PACE® Picante Sauce	½ teaspoon salt
¾ cup quick-cooking oats, uncooked	¼ teaspoon pepper
1 small onion, chopped	6 hamburger buns

Combine all ingredients except buns; mix well. Shape into 6 large patties. Grill or broil to desired doneness. Serve on buns with additional picante sauce. *Makes 6 servings*

Spicy Tuna Empanadas

Rolled Mexican Chicken

8 boneless skinless chicken
   breast halves
   (2 pounds)
1 package (1.25 ounces)
   LAWRY'S® Taco Spices
   & Seasonings, divided
1 cup (4 ounces) shredded
   Monterey Jack cheese

1 can (4 ounces) diced
   green chilies, drained
¼ cup butter or margarine,
   melted or 1 to 2 egg
   whites, slightly beaten
1 bag (8 ounces) tortilla
   chips, crushed

Place chicken breasts between two sheets of waxed paper; pound
to ⅛-inch thickness. In medium bowl, combine 1 tablespoon Taco
Spices & Seasonings, cheese and green chilies. Spread equal
amounts of cheese mixture onto chicken breasts. Roll up chicken
tightly; secure with toothpick.

In shallow baking dish, place melted butter. Roll each chicken
bundle in butter. In second shallow dish or on plate, combine
remaining Taco Spices & Seasonings and tortilla chips. Roll each
chicken bundle in seasoned chips to coat; return to baking dish.
Bake in 350°F oven 30 minutes or until no longer pink and juices
run clear when chicken is cut. Remove from oven; let stand 5
minutes before slicing to serve. Garnish, if desired.

Makes 6 to 8 servings

PRESENTATION: *Serve with Mexicali Rice and Beans (page 34), if
desired.*

Taco Burgers

2 pounds ground beef
1 envelope LIPTON®
   Recipe Secrets® Onion
   Soup Mix

½ cup finely chopped green
   bell pepper
1 medium tomato, chopped
2 teaspoons chili powder

In large bowl, combine all ingredients; shape into 12 oblong
burgers. Grill or broil until meat is no longer pink. Serve, if
desired, in taco shells or frankfurter rolls and top with shredded
lettuce and shredded Cheddar cheese. *Makes 12 servings*

NOTE: *Also terrific with Lipton® Recipe Secrets® Beefy Onion or Beefy
Mushroom Soup Mix.*

Rolled Mexican Chicken

Steak Ranchero

⅔ cup A.1.® Steak Sauce
⅔ cup mild, medium or hot
   thick and chunky salsa
2 tablespoons lime juice

1 (1-pound) beef top round
   steak, about ¾ inch
   thick
⅓ cup sliced ripe olives
4 cups shredded lettuce
⅓ cup dairy sour cream

In small bowl, combine steak sauce, salsa and lime juice. Place steak in glass dish; coat both sides with ½ cup salsa mixture. Cover; chill 1 hour, turning occasionally.

In small saucepan, over medium heat, heat remaining salsa mixture. Reserve 2 tablespoons olives for garnish; stir remaining olives into sauce. Keep warm.

Remove steak from marinade; discard marinade. Grill over medium heat for 6 minutes on each side or until done, turning once.

To serve, arrange lettuce on serving platter. Thinly slice steak across grain; arrange over lettuce. Top with warm sauce and sour cream. Garnish with reserved olive slices.   *Makes 4 servings*

Huevos con Arroz

1 package (6.8 ounces)
   RICE-A-RONI® Spanish
   Rice
2 cups chopped tomatoes
4 eggs
½ cup (2 ounces) shredded
   Cheddar cheese or
   Monterey Jack cheese

2 tablespoons chopped
   fresh cilantro or
   parsley
¼ cup salsa or picante
   sauce (optional)

1. Prepare Rice-A-Roni Mix as package directs, substituting fresh tomatoes for 1 can (14½ ounces) tomatoes. Bring to a boil over high heat. Cover; reduce heat. Simmer 20 minutes.

2. Make 4 round indentations in rice with back of large spoon. Break 1 egg into each indentation. Cover; cook over low heat 5 to 7 minutes or until eggs are cooked. Sprinkle with cheese and cilantro. Top with salsa.   *Makes 4 servings*

Fish Fillets with Green Tomato Salsa

1 pound catfish,* cut into
   4 serving pieces
½ cup prepared chunky
   salsa
2 tomatillos or green
   tomatoes, chopped
   (about ½ cup)

1 tablespoon chopped
   fresh cilantro
2 teaspoons lime juice
¼ teaspoon ground
   coriander
Tortillas

Microwave Directions: Rinse fish and pat dry with paper towels. Arrange in an 8-inch square glass baking dish so that pieces are toward the sides of dish. Combine salsa, tomatillos, cilantro, lime juice and coriander. Spoon mixture over fish. Cover with vented plastic wrap. Microwave on HIGH 3 to 4 minutes or just until fish flakes when tested with a fork, rotating dish midway through cooking. Serve on a heated tortilla garnished with sprigs of cilantro. *Makes 4 servings*

*Snapper, orange roughy or other lean whitefish such as flounder, cod, sole or pollock can also be used.

Favorite recipe from **National Fisheries Institute**

Mexicali Pizzas

2 (9-inch) flour tortillas
2 cups (8 ounces) Monterey
   Jack cheese
1 (16-ounce) can VEG-ALL®
   Mixed Vegetables,
   drained
1 cup chopped tomato

½ cup finely chopped green
   onions
½ cup finely chopped green
   pepper
3 tablespoons mild green
   chilies
¼ cup sliced ripe olives

Place tortillas on lightly greased baking sheet. Sprinkle one tortilla with ½ cup cheese; top with half the Veg-All®, tomato, onions, pepper and chilies. Sprinkle with ½ cup cheese and top with ½ of the olives. Repeat with second tortilla. Bake at 425°F approximately 10 to 12 minutes or until cheese is melted and tortillas are crisp. *Makes 2 (9-inch) pizzas*

Fish Fillets with Green Tomato Salsa

Mexican Frittata

3 tablespoons butter or
    margarine
2 cups (8 ounces) frozen
    ready-to-cook hash
    brown potatoes with
    peppers and onions
    (O'Brien style),
    thawed*
5 eggs

½ cup salsa
¼ teaspoon salt
2 cups (8 ounces)
    SARGENTO® 4 Cheese
    Mexican Recipe Blend,
    divided
Sour cream (optional)
Chopped fresh cilantro
    (optional)

Melt butter in 10-inch ovenproof skillet over high heat. Swirl
butter up side of pan to prevent frittata from sticking. Add
potatoes to skillet; cook 3 minutes, stirring occasionally. Reduce
heat to medium.

Beat eggs in medium bowl. Stir in salsa and salt. Stir in 1 cup of
4 Cheese Mexican Recipe Blend. Add egg mixture to skillet; stir
gently to combine. Cover; cook 6 minutes without stirring or
until eggs are set around edges. (Center will be wet.) Sprinkle
remaining 1 cup cheese evenly over frittata. Place under
preheated broiler 4 to 5 inches from heat source. Broil 2 to 3
minutes or until cheese is melted and eggs are set in center. Cut
into wedges; serve with sour cream and cilantro, if desired.

Makes 4 servings

*To thaw frozen potatoes, microwave at HIGH 2 to 3 minutes.

Layered Mexicali Casserole

1 pound ground beef
1 (16-ounce) can
    ROSARITA® Refried
    Beans
1 (15-ounce) can HUNT'S®
    Tomato Sauce Special
1 (1.25-ounce) package taco
    seasoning mix
6 (8-inch) flour tortillas
1 (14½-ounce) can HUNT'S®
    Choice-Cut Tomatoes,
    drained

¾ cup sliced green onions
1 (4-ounce) can
    ROSARITA® Diced
    Green Chiles
1 (2¼-ounce) can sliced
    ripe olives, drained
4 cups (16 ounces)
    shredded Cheddar
    cheese
Sour cream (optional)
Avocado slices (optional)

In large skillet, brown ground beef; drain. Stir in beans, tomato sauce and taco seasoning. Bring to a boil; reduce heat and simmer 15 minutes. In lightly greased 13 × 9 × 2-inch baking dish, place 2 tortillas side by side on bottom of dish. Spread ⅓ of the meat mixture over tortillas and sprinkle with ⅓ of each of the tomatoes, green onions, chiles, olives and cheese. Repeat layers twice, ending with cheese.

Bake at 350°F for 40 minutes. Let stand 10 minutes before serving. Garnish each serving with sour cream and an avocado slice, if desired. *Makes 8 to 10 servings*

Fiesta Pork Roast

1 (6- to 7-pound) pork loin
   roast
1 tablespoon salt
2 teaspoons onion powder
2 teaspoons garlic powder
½ teaspoon pepper
1½ cups water
8 small whole onions,
   peeled

¾ cup currant jelly
½ teaspoon hot pepper
   sauce
8 small seedless oranges,
   peeled
¼ cup water
3 tablespoons all-purpose
   flour

Combine salt, onion powder, garlic powder and pepper. Sprinkle on pork roast; rub into roast. Place roast in shallow roasting pan; insert meat thermometer. Roast at 325°F for 1 hour. Add 1½ cups water to pan. Place onions around roast. Combine currant jelly and hot pepper sauce; brush on roast and onions. Continue to roast for 1 hour or until meat thermometer registers 155°F to 160°F. Remove roast; let stand 5 to 10 minutes before slicing. Meanwhile, add oranges to hot liquid in pan; heat thoroughly. Remove onions and oranges; keep warm. To make gravy, combine ¼ cup water and flour; mix until smooth. Bring pan liquid to a boil; gradually stir in flour mixture. Cook and stir until thickened. Serve with onions and oranges. *Makes 16 servings*

Favorite recipe from **National Pork Producers Council**

Picadillo Chicken

1 broiler-fryer chicken, cut
   up (about 3½ pounds)
1½ tablespoons all-purpose
   flour
½ teaspoon salt
2 tablespoons vegetable oil
1 large onion, coarsely
   chopped
2 cloves garlic, minced
1 can (14½ ounces) stewed
   tomatoes
1 can (8 ounces) tomato
   sauce
⅓ cup raisins

⅓ cup sliced pickled
   jalapeños, drained
1 teaspoon ground cumin
¼ teaspoon cinnamon
⅓ cup toasted slivered
   almonds
Hot cooked rice
   (optional)
1 cup (4 ounces)
   SARGENTO® Fancy
   Supreme Shredded
   Cheese For Nachos
   & Tacos

Rinse chicken; pat dry. Dust with flour and salt. In large skillet, brown chicken skin side down in hot oil over medium heat, about 5 minutes; turn. Add onion and garlic; cook 5 minutes more. Add stewed tomatoes, tomato sauce, raisins, jalapeños, cumin and cinnamon; heat to a boil. Reduce heat; cover and simmer 15 minutes. Uncover and simmer 5 to 10 minutes more or until chicken is tender and sauce is thickened.* Stir in almonds; serve over rice. Sprinkle with Nachos & Tacos cheese.

Makes 6 servings

*At this point, chicken may be covered and refrigerated up to 2 days before serving. Reheat before adding almonds.

Picadillo Chicken

Ya Gotta Empanada

1 package (4.4 to
6.8 ounces) Spanish
rice mix, prepared
according to package
directions
1 cup shredded cooked
chicken

1 cup (4 ounces) shredded
Cheddar cheese
½ cup sliced green onions
¼ cup chopped black olives
1 package (15 ounces)
refrigerated pie crust

Combine rice, chicken, cheese, onions and olives in large bowl.
Spoon half of rice mixture on half of each pie crust. Fold crust
over filling. Seal and crimp edges. Place on baking sheet. Bake at
400°F 20 to 22 minutes or until golden brown. Cut each
empanada in half. Serve immediately.

Makes 4 servings (½ empanada each)

Favorite recipe from **USA Rice Council**

Ixtapa Stuffed Peppers

4 large red or green bell
peppers
1 pound boneless skinless
chicken breasts, cut
into ¼-inch pieces
½ cup chopped green bell
pepper
½ cup frozen corn or
canned corn, drained

½ cup salsa
1 to 1½ teaspoons chili
powder
½ to 1 teaspoon ground
cumin
4 cups Corn CHEX® brand
cereal

Preheat oven to 350°F. Grease 11 × 7-inch baking dish. Cut
peppers in half lengthwise. Remove and discard stems and seeds;
set pepper halves aside. Combine chicken, chopped green pepper,
corn, salsa, chili powder and cumin; mix well. Add cereal; mix
well. Fill each pepper half with about 1 cup chicken mixture.
Place in prepared baking dish. Bake, covered, 20 minutes;
remove cover and bake an additional 20 to 25 minutes or until
chicken is no longer pink. Top with additional salsa if desired.
Serve immediately.

Makes 4 servings

Ya Gotta Empanada

Sonora Shrimp

2 tablespoons IMPERIAL® Margarine
1 medium green bell pepper, coarsely chopped
½ cup chopped onion
½ cup chopped celery
1 can (14½ ounces) whole peeled tomatoes, undrained and cut up
½ cup dry white wine
½ teaspoon LAWRY'S® Seasoned Salt
½ teaspoon LAWRY'S® Seasoned Pepper
¼ teaspoon LAWRY'S® Garlic Powder with Parsley
¼ teaspoon dried thyme, crushed
1 pound medium shrimp, peeled and deveined
1 can (2¼ ounces) sliced ripe olives, drained

In large skillet, melt margarine and sauté bell pepper, onion and celery. Add remaining ingredients except shrimp and olives; blend well. Bring to a boil; reduce heat and simmer, uncovered, 15 minutes, stirring occasionally. Add shrimp and olives; cook 10 minutes or until shrimp turn pink. *Makes 4 to 6 servings*

PRESENTATION: *Serve over hot fluffy rice.*

Tamale Pie Rancheros

2 tablespoons vegetable oil
¼ cup chopped onion
¼ cup chopped green pepper
¾ pound ground beef
1 (16-ounce) can stewed tomatoes
1 (16-ounce) can VEG-ALL® Mixed Vegetables, drained
1 cup cornmeal
2 tablespoons mild green chilies
1 teaspoon dried basil leaves
⅛ teaspoon black pepper
½ cup (2 ounces) shredded Cheddar cheese

Heat oil in heavy skillet. Add onion and green pepper; cook over low heat until tender. Add ground beef; cook and stir until brown. Stir in tomatoes, Veg-All®, cornmeal, chilies, basil and pepper. Place in 9-inch pie plate and bake at 375°F for 30 to 35 minutes. Top with cheese; bake 5 minutes. *Makes 6 servings*

Sonora Shrimp

Picante Four-Pepper Pasta

8 ounces mostaccioli or
rotini, uncooked
1 large onion, quartered
lengthwise, thinly
sliced crosswise
1 large green pepper, cut
into short, thin strips
1 large red pepper, cut into
short, thin strips
1 large yellow pepper, cut
into short, thin strips

1 tablespoon minced garlic
2 tablespoons olive oil
1 teaspoon dried basil
leaves
½ teaspoon dried oregano
leaves
⅔ cup PACE® Picante Sauce
2 tablespoons balsamic
vinegar
¼ cup grated Parmesan
cheese

Cook pasta according to package directions; drain. While pasta
cooks, cook onion, peppers and garlic in oil in large skillet over
medium-high heat, stirring frequently, 5 minutes. Sprinkle basil
and oregano over vegetables; continue cooking, stirring
frequently, until vegetables are tender, 6 to 7 minutes. Add
picante sauce and vinegar; cook and stir 2 minutes. Spoon pepper
mixture over pasta; sprinkle with cheese. Toss. Serve with
additional cheese, if desired, and additional picante sauce.

Makes 4 to 6 servings

Amigo Pita Pocket Sandwiches

1 pound ground turkey
1 package (1.25 ounces)
LAWRY'S® Taco Spices
& Seasonings
1 can (7 ounces) whole
kernel corn, drained
1 can (6 ounces) tomato
paste

½ cup water
½ cup chopped green bell
pepper
8 pita breads
Curly lettuce leaves
Shredded Cheddar
cheese

In large skillet, brown turkey; drain fat. Add remaining
ingredients except pita bread, lettuce and cheese; blend well.
Bring to a boil; reduce heat and simmer, uncovered, 15 minutes.
Cut off top ¼ of pita breads. Open pita breads to form pockets.
Line each with lettuce leaves. Spoon ½ cup filling into each pita
bread and top with cheese.

Makes 8 servings

Picante Four-Pepper Pasta

Chili Salsa Beef

1½ pounds boneless beef
   chuck shoulder roast
1 tablespoon olive oil
1 cup prepared medium or
   hot chunky salsa
2 tablespoons packed
   brown sugar
1 tablespoon reduced-
   sodium soy sauce

1 clove garlic, crushed
⅓ cup coarsely chopped
   fresh cilantro
2 tablespoons fresh lime
   juice
2 cups cooked rice
   Cilantro sprigs (optional)
1 lime, cut crosswise into
   quarters (optional)

1. Trim fat from beef roast. Cut roast into 1¼-inch pieces. In
Dutch oven, heat oil over medium heat until hot. Add beef and
brown evenly, stirring occasionally. Pour off drippings.

2. Stir salsa, sugar, soy sauce and garlic into beef. Bring to a boil;
reduce heat to low. Cover tightly and simmer 1 hour. Remove
cover; continue cooking, uncovered, an additional 30 minutes or
until beef is tender.

3. Remove from heat; stir in chopped cilantro and lime juice.
Spoon beef mixture over rice; garnish with cilantro sprigs and
lime quarters, if desired. *Makes 4 servings*

Favorite recipe from **National Live Stock & Meat Board**

Nacho Bacho

1½ pounds ground beef
1 cup chunky hot salsa
½ cup salad dressing
2 tablespoons Italian
   seasoning
1 tablespoon chili powder

2 cups (8 ounces) shredded
   Colby-Jack cheese
3 cups nacho-flavored
   tortilla chips, crushed
1 cup sour cream
½ cup sliced black olives

Brown ground beef; drain. In medium bowl, combine salsa, salad
dressing, Italian seasoning and chili powder. Add beef. Place in
11 × 7-inch baking dish. Top with 1 cup cheese. Cover with
crushed chips and remaining cheese. Bake at 350°F 20 minutes.
Garnish with sour cream and sliced olives. *Makes 4 servings*

Favorite recipe from **North Dakota Beef Commission**

Chili Salsa Beef

Southwest Chicken

1 package (6.8 ounces)
RICE-A-RONI® Spanish
Rice
½ cup chopped green bell
pepper *or* 1 can
(4 ounces) chopped
green chilies, drained
1 can (14½ ounces)
tomatoes, undrained,
chopped
⅓ cup QUAKER® or AUNT
JEMIMA® Yellow Corn
Meal

1½ teaspoons chili powder
½ teaspoon garlic powder
4 boneless skinless chicken
breast halves
2 eggs, beaten
3 tablespoons vegetable oil
¼ cup (1 ounce) shredded
Cheddar or Monterey
Jack cheese

1. Prepare Rice-A-Roni Mix as package directs, stirring in green pepper with water and tomatoes.

2. While Rice-A-Roni is simmering, combine corn meal, chili powder and garlic powder. Coat chicken with corn meal mixture; dip chicken into eggs, then coat again with corn meal mixture.

3. In second large skillet, heat oil over medium heat. Add chicken; cook 6 minutes on each side or until golden brown and no longer pink in center.

4. Serve rice topped with chicken; sprinkle with cheese. Cover; let stand a few minutes before serving.   *Makes 4 servings*

Southwest Chicken

Chunky Salsa Chicken Sandwiches

2½ cups diced cooked
  chicken
1 cup DANNON® Plain
  Lowfat Yogurt
¼ cup chunky salsa
½ teaspoon ground cumin
½ cup finely chopped red
  or green bell pepper
⅓ cup finely chopped fresh
  cilantro or parsley

⅓ cup finely chopped green
  onions
3 (6-inch) pita bread
  rounds, cut in half
Toppings: Shredded
  lettuce, sliced ripe
  olives, chopped
  tomatoes and shredded
  Cheddar cheese

In a large bowl combine chicken, yogurt, salsa and cumin; stir
gently. Stir in bell pepper, cilantro and green onions. Line each
pita half with lettuce. Spoon chicken mixture into pockets;
sprinkle remaining toppings over chicken mixture. Serve
immediately.   *Makes 6 servings*

California Tamale Pie

¾ pound ground beef
2½ cups milk
1 cup yellow cornmeal
2 eggs, beaten
1 package (1.62 ounces)
  LAWRY'S® Spices &
  Seasonings for Chili
1 teaspoon LAWRY'S®
  Garlic Salt

1 can (14½ ounces) whole
  tomatoes, cut up
1 can (8 ounces) whole
  kernel corn, drained
1 can (2¼ ounces) sliced
  ripe olives, drained
1½ cups (6 ounces) shredded
  Cheddar cheese
2 tablespoons yellow
  cornmeal

In medium skillet, brown ground beef; drain. In medium bowl,
combine milk, 1 cup cornmeal and eggs; blend well. Add ground
beef and remaining ingredients except cheese and 2 tablespoons
cornmeal; stir to mix. Pour into 12 × 8-inch lightly greased baking
dish. Bake in 350°F oven 35 to 40 minutes. Sprinkle with cheese
and 2 tablespoons cornmeal; continue baking until cheese melts.
Let stand 10 minutes before serving.   *Makes 6 to 8 servings*

Chunky Salsa Chicken Sandwiches

Sausage Stuffed Chicken Breast Olé

6 boneless skinless chicken
breast halves
1 pound BOB EVANS
FARMS® Original
Recipe or Zesty Hot
Roll Sausage
1 (8-ounce) block Monterey
Jack cheese, divided
4 tablespoons butter or
margarine, divided
1 large green bell pepper,
sliced into rings
1 large onion, sliced into
rings

2 cloves garlic, minced
2 (16-ounce) cans stewed
tomatoes, undrained
1 (12-ounce) can large
black olives, drained,
sliced and divided
¼ cup chopped fresh
cilantro
3 tablespoons chopped
jalapeño peppers
(optional)
Sour cream (optional)
Fresh cilantro sprigs
(optional)

Pound chicken into uniform thin rectangles with meat mallet or
rolling pin. Divide uncooked sausage into 6 equal pieces. Cut 6
(½-inch-thick) sticks from cheese block. Shred remaining cheese;
set aside. Wrap each sausage piece around each cheese stick to
enclose cheese completely. Place each sausage bundle on each
chicken piece at one narrow end; roll up and secure with
toothpicks. Melt 2 tablespoons butter in Dutch oven or large
skillet over medium heat until hot. Add chicken bundles; cook,
covered, about 5 to 7 minutes on each side or until browned,
turning occasionally. Remove chicken; set aside.

Melt remaining 2 tablespoons butter in same Dutch oven. Add
bell pepper, onion and garlic; cook and stir until lightly browned.
Stir in tomatoes with juice, half the olives, chopped cilantro and
jalapeños, if desired. Cook and stir over medium-low heat about
10 minutes. Add chicken bundles. Cook, covered, 30 to 40 minutes
or until flavors blend. To serve, spoon tomato sauce mixture on
top of chicken. Sprinkle with remaining cheese and olives, if
desired. Garnish with dollop of sour cream and cilantro sprigs, if
desired. Serve hot. Refrigerate leftovers.   *Makes 6 servings*

Acknowledgments

The publishers would like to thank the companies and organizations listed below for the use of their recipes and photos in this publication.

Bob Evans Farms®
California Table Grape Commission
California Tomato Board
The Dannon Company, Inc.
Dean Foods Vegetable Company
Del Monte Corporation
Farmhouse Foods Company
Florida Department of Agriculture and Consumer Services
Golden Grain/Mission Pasta
Hunt Food Co.
Kraft Foods, Inc.
Lawry's® Foods, Inc.
Thomas J. Lipton Co.
McIlhenny Company
Nabisco Foods Group
National Broiler Council
National Fisheries Institute
National Live Stock & Meat Board
National Pork Producers Council
National Turkey Federation
Nestlé Food Company
Newman's Own, Inc.
North Dakota Beef Commission
Pace Foods, Ltd.
Ralston Foods, Inc.
Sargento Foods Inc.®
StarKist Seafood Company
Surimi Seafood Education Center
USA Dry Pea & Lentil Council
USA Rice Council
Walnut Marketing Board

Index

Acapulco Salad, 27
Albóndigas Soup, 51
Amigo Pita Pocket Sandwiches, 113
Appetizers, *see also* **Salsas**
  Deluxe Fajita Nachos, 9
  Empandillas, 16
  Festive Chicken Dip, 6
  Guacamole, 13
  Independence Day Bean Dip, 17
  Layered Guacamole, 10
  Mexican Chicken Skewers with
    Spicy Yogurt Sauce, 2
  Mexican Chili Walnuts, 23
  Mexi Chex®, 5
  Rio Grande Quesadillas, 13
  South-of-the-Border Sausage Balls,
    16
  Southwestern Seafood Dip, 14
  Spicy Empanadas, 19
  Spicy Taco Dip, 20
Arroz Mexicana, 27
Avocado Orange Soup, 51
Aztec Chili Salad, 31

Baja Beef Enchiladas, 74
Baja Corn Chowder, 56
Baked Citrus Fruit, 84
Bean and Vegetable Burritos, 77
Beef
  Chili Salsa Beef, 114
  Skillet Steak Fajitas, 60
  Steak Ranchero, 100
  Tijuana Blackened Steak, 92
Beef, ground
  Albóndigas Soup, 51
  Aztec Chili Salad, 31
  Baja Beef Enchiladas, 74
  Burgers Olé!, 96
  California Tamale Pie, 118
  Chili Pizza, 92
  Empandillas, 16
  Fiesta Corn Casserole, 35
  Hot Taco Salad, 42
  Layered Mexicali Casserole, 104
  Mexicali Beef & Rice, 95
  Mexi Chex®, 5
  Nacho Bacho, 114
  Quick 'n' Easy Tacos, 83
  Rice & Bean Burritos, 72

Special Beef and Spinach Burritos,
    82
  Spicy Burrito Burgers, 88
  Taco Burgers, 99
  Taco Twist Soup, 47
  Tamale Pie Rancheros, 110
  30-Minute Chili Olé, 56
Black Bean Turkey Pepper Salad, 32
Border Black Bean Chicken Salad, 24
Border Scramble, 64
Breakfast Burritos with Baked Citrus
    Fruit, 84
Breakfast Quesadillas, 68
Breakfast Tacos, 88
Burgers Olé!, 96
Burritos
  Bean and Vegetable Burritos, 77
  Border Scramble, 64
  Breakfast Burritos with Baked
    Citrus Fruit, 84
  Rice & Bean Burritos, 72
  Special Beef and Spinach Burritos,
    82
  Tuna Salad Burritos, 67

California Tamale Pie, 118
Chicken
  Border Black Bean Chicken Salad,
    24
  Chicken Feta Fajitas, 64
  Chunky Salsa Chicken Sandwiches,
    118
  Classic Arroz con Pollo, 90
  Deluxe Fajita Nachos, 9
  Festive Chicken Dip, 6
  Ixtapa Stuffed Peppers, 109
  Mexican Chicken Skewers with
    Spicy Yogurt Sauce, 2
  Picadillo Chicken, 106
  Rio Grande Quesadillas, 13
  Rolled Mexican Chicken, 99
  Salsa Corn Soup with Chicken, 52
  Sausage Stuffed Chicken Breast
    Olé, 120
  South-of-the-Border Chicken Soup,
    59
  Southwest Chicken, 117
  Tex-Mex Chicken & Rice Chili, 52
  Tex-Mex Chicken Fajitas, 78
  Ya Gotta Empanada, 109
Chili Blanco, 47
Chili Pizza, 92
Chili Salsa Beef, 114
Chunky Salsa, 17

Chunky Salsa Chicken Sandwiches, 118
Classic Arroz con Pollo, 90
Corn Salsa, 10
Creamy Gazpacho, 59

Deluxe Fajita Nachos, 9

El Dorado Rice Casserole, 32
Empandillas, 16
Enchiladas
Baja Beef Enchiladas, 74
Enchiladas de Puerco y Frijoles, 82
Enchiladas Fantasticas, 73
Shrimp Enchiladas, 67
Ensenada Fish Tacos, 87

Fajitas
Chicken Feta Fajitas, 64
Fantastic Pork Fajitas, 81
Skillet Steak Fajitas, 60
Tex-Mex Chicken Fajitas, 78
Fantastic Pork Fajitas, 81
Festive Chicken Dip, 6
Fiesta Corn 'n' Peppers, 41
Fiesta Corn Casserole, 35
Fiesta Pork Roast, 105
Fish Fillets with Green Tomato Salsa, 103
Fresh California Tomato-Pineapple Salsa, 5
Fresh Grape Salsa and Chips, 23

Gazpacho Salad, 34
Guacamole, 13

Hot Taco Salad, 42
Huevos con Arroz, 100
Huevos Rancheros Tostados, 71

Independence Day Bean Dip, 17
Ixtapa Stuffed Peppers, 109

Layered Guacamole, 10
Layered Mexicali Casserole, 104

Mexicali Beef & Rice, 95
Mexicali Pizzas, 103
Mexicali Rice and Beans, 34
Mexican Chicken Skewers with Spicy Yogurt Sauce, 2
Mexican Chili Walnuts, 23
Mexican Frittata, 104

Mexican Pork Salad, 42
Mexi Chex®, 5

Nacho Bacho, 114
Nacho Cheese Soup, 55
No Way, José Lentil Salsa, 9

Orange-Chili Glazed Shrimp, 38

Picadillo Chicken, 106
Picante Four-Pepper Pasta, 113
Pork
Enchiladas de Puerco y Frijoles, 82
Fantastic Pork Fajitas, 81
Fiesta Pork Roast, 105
Mexican Pork Salad, 42
Pork Tenderloin Mole, 95
Santa Fe Taco Stew, 44
Tacos Picadillos, 81
Texas Fajita Chili, 55

Quesadillas
Breakfast Quesadillas, 68
Rio Grande Quesadillas, 13
Quick 'n' Easy Tacos, 83
Quick Corn Bread with Chilies 'n' Cheese, 28

Red Chili Tortilla Torte, 72
Rice & Bean Burritos, 72
Rio Grande Quesadillas, 13
Rolled Mexican Chicken, 99

Salads
Acapulco Salad, 27
Aztec Chili Salad, 31
Black Bean Turkey Pepper Salad, 32
Border Black Bean Chicken Salad, 24
Gazpacho Salad, 34
Hot Taco Salad, 42
Mexican Pork Salad, 42
Santa Fe Potato Salad, 41
South-of-the-Border Salad, 37
Spinach Salad with Orange-Chili Glazed Shrimp, 38
Salsa Corn Soup with Chicken, 52
Salsa Italiano, 20
Salsas
Chunky Salsa, 17
Corn Salsa, 10
Fresh California Tomato-Pineapple Salsa, 5

Salsas, *continued*
 Fresh Grape Salsa and Chips, 23
 No Way, José Lentil Salsa, 9
 Salsa Italiano, 20
Santa Fe Potato Salad, 41
Santa Fe Taco Stew, 44
Sausage
 Border Scramble, 64
 Breakfast Quesadillas, 68
 South-of-the-Border Sausage Balls,
 16
 Spicy Taco Dip, 20
 Tacos, 71
Seafood
 Ensenada Fish Tacos, 87
 Fish Fillets with Green Tomato
 Salsa, 103
 Gazpacho Salad, 34
 Orange-Chili Glazed Shrimp, 38
 Shrimp Enchiladas, 67
 Sonora Shrimp, 110
 South-of-the-Border Salad, 37
 Southwestern Seafood Dip, 14
 Spicy Tuna Empanadas, 96
 Spinach Salad with Orange-Chili
 Glazed Shrimp, 38
 StarKist® Vegetable Gazpacho,
 48
 Tuna Fiesta Soft Tacos, 68
 Tuna Salad Burritos, 67
Shrimp Enchiladas, 67
Side Dishes
 Arroz Mexicana, 27
 El Dorado Rice Casserole, 32
 Fiesta Corn 'n' Peppers, 41
 Fiesta Corn Casserole, 35
 Mexicali Rice and Beans, 34
 Quick Corn Bread with Chilies 'n'
 Cheese, 28
 South-of-the-Border Vegetable
 Kabobs, 28
 Upside-Down Corn Bread, 37
Skillet Steak Fajitas, 60
Sonora Shrimp, 110
Soups
 Albóndigas Soup, 51
 Avocado Orange Soup, 51
 Baja Corn Chowder, 56
 Creamy Gazpacho, 59
 Nacho Cheese Soup, 55
 Salsa Corn Soup with Chicken,
 52
 South-of-the-Border Chicken Soup,
 59

 StarKist® Vegetable Gazpacho,
 48
 Taco Twist Soup, 47
 South-of-the-Border Chicken Soup,
 59
 South-of-the-Border Salad, 37
 South-of-the-Border Sausage Balls,
 16
 South-of-the-Border Vegetable
 Kabobs, 28
Southwest Chicken, 117
Southwestern Seafood Dip, 14
Special Beef and Spinach Burritos,
 82
Spicy Bean Tostadas, 63
Spicy Burrito Burgers, 88
Spicy Empanadas, 19
Spicy Taco Dip, 20
Spicy Tuna Empanadas, 96
Spinach Salad with Orange-Chili
 Glazed Shrimp, 38
StarKist® Vegetable Gazpacho, 48
Steak Ranchero, 100

Taco Burgers, 99
Tacos
 Breakfast Tacos, 88
 Ensenada Fish Tacos, 87
 Quick 'n' Easy Tacos, 83
 Tacos, 71
 Tacos Picadillos, 81
 Tuna Fiesta Soft Tacos, 68
 Turkey Tacos, 87
Taco Twist Soup, 47
Tamale Pie Rancheros, 110
Texas Fajita Chili, 55
Tex-Mex Chicken & Rice Chili, 52
Tex-Mex Chicken Fajitas, 78
30-Minute Chili Olé, 56
Tijuana Blackened Steak, 92
Tuna Fiesta Soft Tacos, 68
Tuna Salad Burritos, 67
Turkey
 Amigo Pita Pocket Sandwiches,
 113
 Black Bean Turkey Pepper Salad,
 32
 Chili Blanco, 47
 Enchiladas Fantasticas, 73
 Turkey Tacos, 87

Upside-Down Corn Bread, 37

Ya Gotta Empanada, 109

Notes

Mexican Cooking Basics

Tacos, burritos and enchiladas—once considered exotic foods—are now as familiar as earlier imports of pizza, quiche and egg rolls. Due to the vibrant flavors, enticing textural contrasts and eye-catching colors, Mexican dishes have been readily accepted into our everyday menus. Mexican cuisine is much more diverse than the taco lover might suspect. Foods native to the region such as corn, tomatoes, beans and chilies have shaped the flavors and textures of many of the familiar dishes. Although traditional Mexican food is often quite spicy, you may find that you prefer your meals hotter or milder. The following gives some tips for altering the heat of a dish as well as a glossary of typical Mexican ingredients.

Chili Peppers

There are over 100 varieties of chilies in Mexico, each with its own unique characteristics. They are used both fresh and dried and dried chilies can be either whole or ground. The heat of chilies comes from the seeds, the veins (the thin inner membranes to which the seeds are attached) and in the parts nearest the veins. For milder dishes, the veins and seeds should be removed and discarded. For more heat, include all or some of the seeds and membranes.

A Note of Caution: The seeds and membranes of dried and fresh chilies contain oils that can cause painful burning if they make contact with your skin, lips or eyes. Wear rubber gloves if you are sensitive to chili pepper oils or if you are handling a number of chilies at one time. Do not touch your face while handling chilies and wash your hands well in warm soapy water after handling.

Fresh chilies will keep for several weeks in a plastic bag lined with paper towels. (The towels absorb any moisture.) When purchasing fresh chilies, select those that have firm, unblemished skin. Jalapeño peppers are the most common fresh chili. They are small and dark green, normally 2 to 3 inches long and about ¾ inch wide with a blunt or slightly tapered end. Their flavor varies from hot to very hot. They are also sold in cans and jars and may be whole, sliced, chopped or pickled.

Dried red chilies are usually sold in cellophane packages of various weights. They will keep indefinitely if stored in a tightly covered container in a cool, dark, dry place.

Mexican Ingredients

Cilantro: An extremely pungent herb with green delicate leaves, similar in appearance, but not flavor, to flat-leaf parsley. Used extensively in Mexican cooking, there is no substitute. Store it in the refrigerator for up to one week with the stems in a glass of water; cover the leaves with a plastic bag.

Chili powder: A blend of spices that may include mild chili peppers, garlic, oregano, salt, cumin, coriander and cloves. It has a spicy taste and can be mild or hot. As with all spices, chili powder should be stored in a cool, dark place for no longer than six months.

Cumin: A small, amber-colored seed that is the dried fruit of a plant in the parsley family. Also known by its Spanish name, *comino,* it has an aromatic, nutty and slightly bitter flavor. It is available as seeds or ground.

Jicama: A root vegetable with thin, tan-brown skin and crisp, sweetish, white flesh. Shaped like a large turnip, jicama is most often used raw in salads or eaten as a refreshing snack. It should be peeled before using. Store it in the refrigerator for up to five days.

Tortillas: The mainstay of Mexican cuisine, these thin, flat breads are made with corn or wheat flour. Tortillas are readily available at supermarkets in the ethnic or refrigerated sections. Corn tortillas usually measure between 5 and 6 inches in diameter; flour tortillas are available in many sizes, ranging from 7 to 12 inches in diameter.

To soften and warm corn or flour tortillas, stack the tortillas and wrap in foil. Heat the stack in a 350°F oven 10 minutes or until the tortillas are warm. To warm them in a microwave, stack the tortillas and wrap them in plastic wrap. Microwave on HIGH ½ to 1 minute, turning them over and rotating ¼ turn once during heating.

METRIC CONVERSION CHART

VOLUME MEASUREMENTS (dry)

⅛ teaspoon = 0.5 mL
¼ teaspoon = 1 mL
½ teaspoon = 2 mL
¾ teaspoon = 4 mL
1 teaspoon = 5 mL
1 tablespoon = 15 mL
2 tablespoons = 30 mL
¼ cup = 60 mL
⅓ cup = 75 mL
½ cup = 125 mL
⅔ cup = 150 mL
¼ cup = 175 mL
1 cup = 250 mL
2 cups = 1 pint = 500 mL
3 cups = 750 mL
4 cups = 1 quart = 1 L

VOLUME MEASUREMENTS (fluid)

1 fluid ounce (2 tablespoons) = 30mL
4 fluid ounces (½ cup) = 125 mL
8 fluid ounces (1 cup) = 250 mL
12 fluid ounces (1½ cups) = 375 mL
16 fluid ounces (2 cups) = 500 mL

WEIGHTS (mass)

½ ounce = 15 g
1 ounce = 30 g
3 ounces = 90 g
4 ounces = 120 g
8 ounces = 225 g
10 ounces = 285 g
12 ounces = 360 g
16 ounces = 1 pound = 450 g

DIMENSIONS

1/16 inch = 2 mm
⅛ inch = 3 mm
¼ inch = 6 mm
½ inch = 1.5 cm
¾ inch = 2 cm
1 inch = 2.5 cm

OVEN TEMPERATURES

250°F = 120°C
275°F = 140°C
300°F = 150°C
325°F = 160°C
350°F = 180°C
375°F = 190°C
400°F = 200°C
425°F = 220°C
450°F = 230°C

BAKING PAN SIZES

Utensil	Size in Inches/ Quarts	Metric Volume	Size in Centimeters
Baking or Cake Pan (square or rectangular)	8×8×2	2 L	20×20×5
	9×9×2	2.5 L	22×22×5
	12×8×2	3 L	30×20×5
	13×9×2	3.5 L	33×23×5
Loaf Pan	8×4×3	1.5 L	20×10×7
	9×5×3	2 L	23×13×7
Round Layer Cake Pan	8×1½	1.2 L	20×4
	9×1½	1.5 L	23×4
Pie Plate	8×1¼	750 mL	20×3
	9×1¼	1 L	23×3
Baking Dish or Casserole	1 quart	1 L	—
	1½ quart	1.5 L	—
	2 quart	2 L	—